LOOKING FOR
THE
GOOD LIFE

LOOKING FOR THE GOOD LIFE

THE SEARCH FOR FULFILLMENT IN THE LIGHT OF ECCLESIASTES

Gordon J. Keddie

Presbyterian and Reformed Publishing Company
Phillipsburg, New Jersey

Manufactured in the United States of America.
Typesetting by Thoburn Press, Box 2459, Reston, Virginia 22090.

Library of Congress Cataloging-in-Publication Data

Keddie, Gordon J., 1944-
    Looking for the good life : the search for fulfillment in the light of Ecclesiastes / Gordon J. Keddie.
        p.   cm.
    Includes bibliographical references.
    ISBN 0-87552-295-5
    1. Bible. O.T. Ecclesiastes—Criticism, interpretation, etc.
2. Bible. O.T. Ecclesiastes—Study.   I. Title.
BS1475.2.K43   1991
223'.807—dc20   90-44341

96   95   94   93   92   91   5   4   3   2   1

CONTENTS

Whereas other civilisations have been brought down by attacks of barbarians from without, ours had the unique distinction of training its own destroyers at its own educational institutions and for providing them with facilities for propagating their destructive ideology far and wide, all at the public expense. Thus did western man decide to abolish himself, creating his own boredom out of his own affluence, his own vulnerability out of his own strength, his own impotence out of his own erotomania, himself blowing the trumpet that brought the walls of his own city tumbling down and, having convinced himself that he was too numerous, laboured with pill and scalpel and the syringe to make himself fewer, until at last, having educated himself into imbecility and polluted and drugged himself into stupefaction, he heeled over: a weary, battered, old Brontosaurus and became extinct.

Malcolm Muggeridge

Better one handful with tranquility
than two handfuls with toil
and chasing after the wind.

Ecclesiastes 4:6

PREFACE

We live in a death-wish society.[1] Secular man has one life to live, a few short years to "make it" in life. And he must live according to the canons of a humanism that has no more to offer than materialist comfort now (if you are American or "lucky") and a lustrous place in the collective consciousness of mankind later (if you can make your mark in history)! While a certain kind of hope attends such expectations for some people, there are many more who see only the prospect of losing out in the end. More and more people are spiraling downward into personal pessimism. In Europe especially, but also increasingly in this traditional "land of opportunity," the United States, you can see it in people's faces. In 1981, after over a decade of living in the United States, I went home to minister in my native Scotland. What struck me most forcibly—even more than the endless wet and windy weather—was the worry etched on the faces of young and old alike. It was like nothing I remembered from the first quarter century of my life over there. There was little of the optimism that still generally prevails in the United States. But what caused this mass anxiety that was so deeply etched on millions of faces? Certainly, the threat of nuclear holocaust was palpably near in Europe. The Chernobyl nuclear disaster brought this home very personally when it made our milk and vegetables radioactive. More pervasive perhaps was the reality of double-digit inflation and unemployment, which had, in practice, condemned a whole generation to a future as a welfare underclass. The sad reality was that a significant proportion of the population was sinking beneath the waves of a nagging hopelessness about life and the future. That "death in the city" which Francis Schaeffer exposed and explained so prophetically over twenty years ago[2] has actually been the formative environment for people under thirty years of age today. The chickens have come home to roost. The mad slogan of a Spanish Civil War leader named Millan Astray, "Long live death,"[3] bids to become the watchword of our time. Why? Because it is in our time that millions of unborn babies are sacrificed by abortion on the altar of career success and personal convenience. It is in our time that a society exists that does not want children and therefore prefers to live out an artificial present that has no future at all. It is in our time that motorists on the California freeways are being gunned down at random and child molestation is the fastest growing criminal offense. Not least, it is in our time that the scourge of AIDS casts its terrifying shadow across the moral, social, and political landscape like a modern version of the medieval plagues! It is in our time that a man awoke in his motel room to find his casual partner of the night before gone — but, in lipstick on the mirror, the macabre valediction, "Welcome to the world of AIDS!"

It must be said however, that most people are not nihilists. There is a very widespread hunger for life and for a happy future. In practice, people who otherwise have no God and no hope in the world are still looking for the good life. They just "keep on keeping on" and leave awkward thoughts about the meaning of it all to a more convenient season (cf. Acts 24:25). But, also in practice, they continue steadfastly to live out of a conventional wisdom that is ever more obviously bankrupt and creeping ever nearer to temporal and eternal disaster. Even the values that order secular society and energize such optimism as is possible for people who believe that dust is the ultimate and absolute end of every human life are all built on the shifting sand of the 51-percent majority—the prevailing consensus of man-centered wisdom. English theologian Alan Richardson was surely correct when he said that "belief in the objectivity of value is the condition of the progress or even of the continuance of civilization." Society could not but perish, "if the generality of men ceased to believe that truth is knowable and moral values binding."⁴ The deepening pessimism of the Western world is a reflection of this spiritual rootlessness.

There are always two ways in which Christians can respond to such a situation. We can keep our heads down, try to survive and pray that the Lord will deliver us in the nick of time (if not before!). This tacitly acknowledges that we believe our pessimism to be fully justified and probably God's program for the contemporary scene.

But there is another way. A good illustration of it is the story of two Christian ministers traveling by train a century or more ago through the north of England. As they drew into Newcastle-upon-Tyne—the place to which it was and still is proverbially silly to take coals—one of the men, seeing the Dickensian squalor, remarked that the place was "ripe for judgment." The other, however, demurred. Said he, "No, this place is ripe for revival." In other words, conquest for Christ, as opposed to survival pending Christ's return, is the appropriate aspiration for Christians even in the face of a sad world beset with what look suspiciously like insuperable problems. Where sin abounds, says Paul, grace much more abounds (Rom. 5:20). The Lord marches toward, not away from, the sound of Satan's gunfire! There is a "good life," and it is the gift of God to those who love him and follow him as his disciples.

I believe that the Book of Ecclesiastes connects with this wonderful and thoroughly biblical notion. Ecclesiastes has been called "pessimism literature," a fitting message from God for our spiritually rootless age. The writer speaks from the contemporary perspective. He questions, even ridicules, the status quo with merciless verve. Then having gotten inside jaundiced minds, he turns our cynicism on its head to point us to the only way of meaningful life. It is a masterly tour de force—a divinely inspired bait-and-switch apologetic that carries the reader from the edge of hell to the threshold of heaven. It is true, as Michael Eaton has observed, that Ecclesiastes is not a work of "full-orbed evangelism." It is, "the opening sentences of an evangelistic message, leading to faith along a pathway of conviction of need. [The writer] asks everyman, starting with the same building material, whether he has learnt to cope with *this* life as it really is."[5] It is, in other words, a kind of preevangelism. The author climbs into the boots of the other fellow—the one who is in the rat race of life "under the sun" and who feels, in a confused kind of way, that it is "meaningless" and "a chasing after wind." At first, Qoheleth—the inspired writer of Ecclesiastes—muses about it all from the godless unbelieving standpoint and so touches a chord with the folk who are depressed and despairing over their own emptiness but don't know how lost they really are—or, more important, where to go for some real meaning, some real truth, some intelligible future. Then, as time goes on and the argument unfolds, the claims of God are unveiled little by little, rising to a climactic appeal to the young to remember their Creator before the decrepitude of age and the finality of death overwhelm them.

In the context of the New Testament, such a message is less than the gospel of Jesus Christ, and yet it marvelously prepares the way for the preaching of Christ as the one whom our Father-God—the Creator we are to remember in the days of our youth (Eccles. 12:1)— has sent to reconcile us to himself through the cross. Ecclesiastes calls us to new life: that life is in Jesus Christ, who came "when the time had fully come" (Gal. 4:4). Because of these truths, the time has come for us to *live* in Jesus our Savior.

Gordon J. Keddie
State College, Pennsylvania

PART ONE
BASICS

1

WHAT'S THE USE?

Please Read Ecclesiastes 1:1-11

> "Meaningless! Meaningless!"
> says the Teacher.
> "Utterly meaningless!
> Everything is meaningless."
> What does man gain from all his labor
> at which he toils under the sun?
>
> Ecclesiastes 1:2-3

Oh God! I'm so bored," read the note found with the body of the former movie star. He was old. His career was over. The reruns on television served only to remind him of a lost youth, of vanished vigor and the memory of a place in the limelight. What had seemed meaningful for his life had been entirely transient and had dissolved into the most bitter emptiness. There was nothing left. He was bored stiff by it all. So he had taken his own life.

Despair is the cancer of the soul. A life without real purpose is a life that is practically over. The contemporary rising tide of despair, frustration, violence, drunkenness, drug death, and suicide crashes with a morbid eloquence over the empty glitz of Western society and insistently challenges us with leading questions about the meaning of life: "What's the use?" "Why bother?" "Who cares?" "What is there to live for?" One twelve-year-old Scottish girl had her answer to these questions. She was interviewed in the street by a television reporter, who asked if she was worried about the damage her smoking habit was doing to her lungs and heart. "Naw," she said, "we're a' goan tae die ony way!" Eat, drink, and be merry, for tomorrow we die!

The problem of the meaning of life is not new. From the beginning, men have been aware of the transience of life and its achievements. The poet Shelley expressed this gnawing reality in his sonnet, "Ozymandius."

> I met a traveller from an antique land
> Who said: Two vast and trunkless legs of stone
> Stand in the desert . . . Near them on the sand,
> Half sunk, a shattered visage lies, whose frown
> And wrinkled lip, and sneer of cold command,
> Tell that its sculptor well those passions read
> Which yet survive, stamped on these lifeless things,
> The hand that mocked them, and the heart that fed:
> And on the pedestal these words appear:
> "My name is Ozymandius, king of kings:
> Look on my works, ye Mighty, and despair!"
> Nothing beside remains. Round the decay
> Of that colossal wreck, boundless and bare
> The lone and level sands stretch far away.[1]

Man's best efforts seem little more than pretensions waiting for a fall. "The paths of glory," as the poet Gray observed, "lead but to the grave."

Everyone recognizes that the Bible is concerned from cover to cover with the meaning of life. Deep in the Old Testament, however, the short Book of Ecclesiastes presents a specific focus on this perennial question. It is an "open letter" from God to everyone who is willing to think about the issues of life. In a graphic and relentless way, the awful realities are exposed—and the way is pointed to God's answers. The result is that we have a word, like no other even in Scripture, that speaks to the "post-Christian" society in which we live. Millennia old, Ecclesiastes is as fresh as the dew. The Teacher[2]—for that is what the eponymous writer's name, "Ecclesiastes" (or *Qoheleth*) means—addresses this message to his own generation with its own particular needs. Israel at that time was in a bad way. Subject to a foreign power—Persia—and wracked internally by moral and spiritual decay, there was a hopelessness and despair abroad in the land.[3] Qoheleth was the bearer of the light of God to the covenant people of the Old Testament to lead them back to the joy of meaningful life in reconciled fellowship with their Savior God. He asked all the basic questions that wracked the minds of men and women in his day. And just as surely and as timely, his message impacts on the need of our own day. Is there any real meaning in life? Or is everything meaningless? This is the issue Qoheleth grapples with to which he brings to bear the very answers of the living God!

Is Everything Meaningless? (1:2)

"Meaningless, meaningless!" says the Teacher, "Utterly meaningless! Everything is meaningless" (1:2). This is a classic cri de coeur – a cry from the heart that feels itself sinking in a maelstrom of frustration and unrelieved gloom. The accumulated despair of the whole world seems to well up within his soul. He feels what they ought to feel. He expresses the pain that they suppress. It is as if he just can't take it anymore. He must bring men and women to their senses. Don't they see? Why do they go on pretending that their miserable earthbound lives are meaningful? It's all a meaningless charade!

On the face of it, Qoheleth seems to be promoting the idea that everything really is meaningless. We must remember, however, that he is constructing an argument designed to lead us from one way of thinking to another that is radically different. He therefore starts with the wrong idea so that he may lead us to the right one. He means to expose what we nowadays call the secular view of life: a life without any absolutes, a life without the certainties of the revelation of God's Word, a life lived out of values generated by man without reference to God, a life that expects lasting satisfaction from earthbound things. Qoheleth wants to show how such a life has to be meaningless and must end in disillusionment in time, not to mention eternity. To heighten the drama of his argument, he gives vivid presentation of this position as if it is all there is!

Surprisingly perhaps, this theme of meaninglessness is only a means to his primary goal. Later, as he develops his argument, he shows his readers that there is real meaning in life and that it consists in loving God and being his disciples (12:13-14). Qoheleth is not a cynic. He firmly believes that all meaning comes from the infinite, personal God who has revealed himself to humanity in his Word. Consequently, he is persuaded that this meaning is only understood and grasped in a personal relationship with God—a living faith in him that issues in a commitment to discipleship as a child of God.

For this reason we must define our terms carefully. What does Qoheleth mean when he ascribes a prima facie meaninglessness to everything? He is not talking in academic jargon to an audience of professional philosophers; he is, rather, addressing the everyday perceptions of thinking men and women. His point of contact with everyone who reads his words is their everyday experience of life.

Everybody experiences the changes and passages of life. Transience, and with it an implication of futility, clings to so much that we do and so much that happens around us in the world. The Bible brings this out repeatedly. "What is your life?" asks James. "You are a mist that appears for a little while and then vanishes" (James 4:14). The creation itself, wrote the apostle Paul, "was subjected to frustration" (Rom. 8:20). And over against the fleeting futility of cosmic impermanence, stands the majestic immutability of the infinite and eternal God and, not least, the promise of redemption. The psalmist felt this very keenly and expressed it most touchingly in Psalm 102:

> Do not take me away, O my God, in the midst of my days;
> your years go on through all generations.
> In the beginning, you laid the foundations of the earth,
> and the heavens are the work of your hands.
> They will perish, but you remain;
> they will all wear out like a garment.
> Like clothing you will change them
> and they will be discarded.
> But you remain the same,
> and your years will never end.
> The children of your servants will live in your presence;
> their descendants will be established before you (vv. 24-28).

Everything around us reminds us of our transient foothold on planet Earth, and only a faith that sees beyond this level of reality can find comfort and security, or even meaning itself, that transcend the inevitabilities of change, decay, and death.

The Hebrew word *hebel* ("meaningless") is used no fewer than thirty-six times in Ecclesiastes. It basically means "wind" or "breath," but, depending upon the specific context, it connotes vanity, senselessness, and transitoriness.[4] This sense of futility attaches to just about every aspect of our lives: pleasure (2:1-2); property (2:4); knowledge (2:12-16); wealth (2:8; 5:8-15); work (2:17-23); success (4:13-16); youth (11:10); and, needless to say, frustration (4:4, 7-8), loneliness (4:9-12), and death (3:19; 11:8). Futility is endemic to the human condition and is inevitably a recurring theme in our experience. Furthermore, if this life is all there is and all we have to look forward to, then what might otherwise have been episodic attacks of a sense of meaninglessness become the underlying irreducible fact of human existence. From such a perspective, people may live only because they would rather not die— a considerable reason, to be sure, but one without a demonstrable hope or significant goal. But to be without God "in the world" inevitably means to be "without hope" (Eph. 2:12). Even if we have a kind of hope in Christ "only for this life"—that is, a purely existential, psychological pseudo-Christianity that has no actual redemption beyond the grave—"we are to be pitied more than all men" (I Cor. 15:19). This outlook sees human history as a track relay race, in which one generation passes on the baton of meaning to the next. Having then run its course, each generation, like Pheidippides after his legendary run between Marathon and Athens, sinks lifeless into the dust of the past evolution of the species. It is all journey and no destination. The goal is to keep on and, somehow, to discover some value in the process itself. Meaning is inevitably bound up with positive self-actualization now and the hope of leaving the world a better place after we've vanished.

Surely this is why pantheistic monism—New Age teaching—is increasingly appealing to a godless, futureless generation.[5] If *now* is all there is, you can be sure that as much meaning as possible will be wrung from it. Why? Because there is no other source! But this source is identical with the "everything" that Qoheleth so emphatically declares to be "utterly meaningless!"

Three Facts of Life (1:3-11)

Strong statements always engender decisive response: people either think hard or they walk away . . . fast! Before we can reject his dramatic proposition out of hand as, perhaps, the raving of a disturbed personality, the writer confronts us with a very down-to-earth question: "What does man gain from all his labor at which he toils under the sun?" (1:3). The key expression is *under the sun*. Used twenty-five times in Ecclesiastes, this phrase characterizes the secularized life as seen through Qoheleth's eyes. And what does it mean? Just that a life limited to material, earthly categories—a life without the eternal dimension and the ultimate reality of the infinite, personal God—is a life lived "under the sun" from beginning to end. What you see is what you get! Nothing more . . . but, sometimes, a lot less! Ask yourself, then, what gain there is in a life lived only under the sun.

Many people, like the miner in the song, feel their lives to be another case of "Sixteen tons, and what do you get? Another day older and deeper in debt." For every "winner" in this life, there are multitudes who think of themselves as "losers" and are assailed daily with a deep sense of discontent and declining expectations. If material or career advancement is the measure of human self-worth and of the meaning of life and labor, how can it be any other way? What we can *gain* becomes the only conceivable palliative to a short life that ends in the dusty anonymity of the grave. Such amelioration may be no more than an existential moment of comfort and meaning—akin, perhaps, to the proverbially sumptuous last meal of the condemned prisoner prior to his execution. But take it away and you take away the only reason some people have for living! Jesus pointedly asks us, "What good is it for a man to gain the whole world, yet forfeit his soul?" (Mark 8:36). Modern secular man replies, "What use is my soul, if I can't have even a little piece of this world?" For him, there is only that which is under the sun. He therefore cannot see the point that Jesus is making. He aches for satisfaction and lasting achievement but is confronted by the same disturbing facts of life at every turn.

Life Is Short (1:4)

"Generations come and generations go, but the earth remains forever" (1:4). Even against the measure of the planet Earth and the elements—never mind eternity—we are here today and gone tomorrow. If you want evidence, just consider the very sun under which you live. The sun, the wind, and the streams continue to function day after day, generation after generation. Finite as the natural world is, it might as well be eternal compared to the life span of a human being. Life is incontrovertibly short. Like Paul Baumer, the hero of Erich Maria Remarque's novel, *All Quiet on the Western Front*, we all live on "the borders of death."[6] The very largeness of the creation around us is a constant proof of our frailty and our transience.

There Is No Lasting Satisfaction (1:8)

"All things are wearisome, more than one can say" (1:8a). If all we have is our sense-world—what we see and hear (1:8b)—we know that there is no end to the round of pleasing our senses. Just as our eyes and ears demand to be fed with new sensations, so an under-the-sun life is never satisfied. Yet the modern consumer society is largely built on this frantic foundation! From the minarets of Madison Avenue to the hoardings and television commercials of the nation's media-ways, it cries, "There is no god but Consumption, and the ad-men are his prophets!" For all the glossy promises, it remains a fact of experience that the highest sensations of the cult of consumerism tend to leave an aftertaste of dissatisfaction and a craving for newer and better experiences. Nowhere has this been more evident than in the rise of the drug culture. A whole generation, jaded and repelled by the emptiness of their parents' materialism, turned for satisfaction to the joys of marijuana, LSD, and sexual freedom. The Rolling Stones' epochal hit of June 1965, "(I Can't Get No) Satisfaction," took what had hitherto been thought and insinuated and blasted it out brazenly as the only way to go! "There they stood," writes Davin Seay, "bad boy superstars seeping disdain . . . hammering out a thundering slab of pig-iron rock 'n' roll, drenched with . . . not innuendo, not smirking entendre . . . but up-front sexual frustration as a metaphor for the whole

appalling specter of a bite-the-hand-that-feeds-'em youth revolt."[7]
Drug deaths and the AIDS plague have bitten deep into the now
middle-aged "sixties youthquake," but the frustration only deepens.
There is no lasting satisfaction under the sun.

There Is Nothing New (1:9-11)

From my six years in George Heriot's School, Edinburgh, Scotland, I can recall vividly two of the many things that our "R.E."
(religious education) teacher, Rev. Joe Graham, attempted to teach
us. One was the story of his seminary classmate, Eric Liddell, the
Scottish missionary and 1924 Olympic champion at 400 meters—
more recently the hero of the movie, *Chariots of Fire*. "Holy Joe," as
Mr. Graham was inevitably nicknamed, waxed unforgettably eloquent when telling of his famous friend. *There* was a man who had
life in its proper biblical proportion and who counted faithfulness
to God of greater value than the Olympic 100 meter gold medal!

The other memorable point was about sin. "Sin," said Holy Joe,
"is first novelty, then drudgery, and finally slavery." I have never
forgotten that, probably because I have found it, from bitter experience, to be such a melancholy truth. And what is true of sin is
true of life in general, as lived under the sun. There is "nothing
new under the sun" (1:9). In other words, what is new never remains new; it soon becomes old hat. In terms of the deeper things
of the human spirit—meaning and aspirations—there is no real
hope of anything different or better. Today's novelty becomes
tomorrow's drudgery and seems, in the end, only to compound the
problem. The promise and benefits of nuclear physics raise the
specter of nuclear holocaust; medical research into problems of in-
fertility leads into the ethical minefield of abortion and genetic
engineering. Today, there is plenty of change, an endless flow of
new things. But what is really new, in terms of the things that matter? In the ancient world, of course, there was a certain timeless-
ness to the passing of the years. The original readers of Ecclesiastes
did not generally experience the kind of rapid change that we today find so commonplace and so impossibly difficult to catch up
with. The force of Qoheleth's words is perhaps blunted by the very
pace of modern society. We are, after all, submerged in novelty as a

matter of everyday experience. Candid reflection, however, un-masks the illusion. Modern man knows in his heart that if any-thing has changed, it has probably been for the worse rather than the better. At the root of the matter, secular man views the world and human history as a closed system. There is no God and no divine goal for life or history. All that remains is unaided human effort clawing forward in the context of an evolving material universe. If the new soon becomes tedious commonplace (1:10), the past becomes irrelevant and slips into forgottenness (1:11). History is bunk. Reality is now. Existence is all. Therefore secular man is unavoidably an existentialist. *Now* is all he has. But *now* is a bore. What, therefore, does he gain under the sun?

Another Way

Qoheleth's readers knew that there was another way. They were, for example, aware that God had created the world and declared it to be good (Gen. 1:10, 18, 21, 25, 31; Pss. 19:1-6; 97:6). They under-stood that sin had entered the world and marred its every aspect and operation to a significant degree. They recognized that it was in the fallenness of the world that death, frustration, and meaning-lessness had their origin. This was the message of Moses and the prophets, who also proclaimed redemption for mankind and renovation of the creation itself (Isa. 11:6-9; 65:17-25). They knew that Qoheleth was speaking for God and pointing to a better way. With New Testament fullness, this promise of redemption comes to the hopelessness felt by so many in our time. The apostle Paul tells us that "the creation waits in eager expectation for the sons of God to be revealed" and declares that the whole of created reality will be "brought into the glorious freedom of the children of God" (Rom. 8:19-21).

There is an alternative to "meaninglessness." It is to see the world God's way. It is to realize your need of a Savior and to come to him in the person of the Lord Jesus Christ, whose death effects the redemption of the lost who will come to him. Christ is the locus of all meaning for a fallen world. Life without a personal faith rela-tionship to him—secular life—is life without ultimate meaning. It is life without a future: rather, more accurately, it is life with a non-

future of eternal alienation from God. Such life in the present is
without true meaningfulness, however much it is overlaid by the
pursuit of knowledge or pleasure. Such life is Ozymandius revisited.
But Jesus calls us, in the good news of his everlasting gospel, to new
life in him—to fullness of meaning—right now and forevermore.

Questions for Discussion

1. The word "meaningless" is used thirty-six times in Ecclesiastes. What activities are declared to be meaningless, and why, in
2:1; 2:4; 2:17-23; 4:4, 7-8; 4:9-12; 4:13-16; 5:8-15; 11:8; 11:10?

2. What is meant by the expression "under the sun"? How does
that compare with what Paul says in I Corinthians 15:19 and Ephe-
sians 2:12? If this life is all there is, why is it "meaningless"?

3. What three facts of life in verses 4, 8, and 9 point to the meaninglessness of life "under the sun"? Apply this to modern life.

4. What are the alternatives to an under-the-sun life? Discuss
some modern solutions to the problem. What does God say about
this world and our life—where it all came from (Ps. 19:1-6); how
he views it (Gen. 1:10, 18, 21); and where it is going (Isa. 65:17-25;
Rom. 8:19-20)?

2
LIFE'S DEAD ENDS
Please Read Ecclesiastes 1:12-2:26

I thought to myself, "Look, I have grown and increased in wisdom more than anyone who has ruled over Jerusalem before me; I have experienced much of wisdom and knowledge." Then I applied myself to the understanding of wisdom, and also of madness and folly, but I learned that this, too, is a chasing after the wind.

Ecclesiastes 1:16-17

Forget everything you've learned in high school," said the professor to the freshmen chemistry class, "it's fifty years out of date!" Allowing for the usual dramatic license, there is a profound practical truth in this piece of academic braggadocio. *Unlearning* is often a necessary precursor to genuine progress in one's eduction. C. S. Lewis saw it in terms of knocking down forests to irrigate deserts. Something may need to be undone before anything new can be achieved. We saw a wonderful example of this when we lived near Glasgow, Scotland. A major hotel had been gutted by fire and plans had been made for its reconstruction. The hotel had taken up most of a magnificent Victorian terrace, in which the many former private homes had been adapted for use as a hotel. The facade was protected because of its historic architectural significance. It could not be replaced by a concrete and glass skyscraper. Rebuilding the outmoded interior was, however, equally impossible, simply because modern facilities had to be provided for the business to become viable once more. The result was a compromise of the best of the past with the best of the present. The stone facade was restored to its original Victorian splendor and behind it, virtually the whole length of a city block, a completely new building was constructed from scratch, to the most rigorous modern specifications!

This, in a nutshell, is the basic method of the writer of Ecclesiastes. He means to break us down in order to build us up—the right way. And so he leads us down the dark corridors of life's dead ends. He faces us with the consequences of a life that has no time for God. He exposes the depressing realities of life under the sun to destroy our happiest illusions and so bring us, like the prodigal son in Jesus' parable (Luke 15:11-32), to our senses—and, thereby, to repentance, reconciliation, and a life of renewal. The lost son had to lose everything before he would face the fact that he had reduced himself to a lower state than the pigs he was employed to feed! He had to unlearn the fantasies that hitherto had been his guiding lights. Only then could he begin life afresh as the son of his father.

Qoheleth, having established the general theme that everything under the sun is utterly meaningless, begins to speak in the first person. He speaks from personal experience. More pointedly, he comes at us from the viewpoint of Solomon, putatively the wisest man in Israel's history (1:12). The reason for this literary ploy is obvious. Who could gainsay the words of such a man? To invoke Solomon was to assert unchallengeable authority. In modern terms, Solomon was "the expert." He was the man with the most distinguished personal bibliography in the field of practical wisdom. Solomon was Mr. Wisdom Literature! Qoheleth uses this literary device quite openly and honestly. He is not that great king of Israel, but he speaks, as he is led by the inspiration of the Spirit of God, as Solomon *redivivus!* He is the second Solomon. Both the man and the century are different, but the teaching is the same.[1] He says, "I devoted myself to study and to explore by wisdom all that is done under heaven" (1:13a). He *thought*—and he thought *long* —about life. He faced facts and searched his soul. Derek Kidner aptly likens this to the intense personal reflections of the apostle Paul in Romans 7. "Each of these two confessions," writes Kidner, "has a wider reference than to the one man who is speaking. Between them, Qoheleth and Paul explore for us man's outer and inner worlds: his search for meaning and his struggle for moral victory."[2]

Knowledge Numbs (1:13b-18)

The teacher looked at his high school history class. In his hand he had the graded papers from their most recent test. The grades were less than wonderful. Adverting to this fact, he shook his head and said, with a genial chuckle, "I've taught you all I know, and you still know nothing." We tenth graders took this as a huge joke: obviously, we reasoned, if our teacher knew nothing and taught us all he knew, we were bound to know nothing! Mature reflection in later life sees another, less amusing, side to these words: the more we learn, the more we see how ignorant we are. In global terms, the advance of human knowledge and, for example, technological achievement, has not issued in a new age of arcadian sweetness and light. Knowledge per se has not produced heaven on earth under the sun! Two facts had impressed themselves upon Qoheleth's experience.

Study Can Be a Real Drag (1:13b-15)

Philosophers and politicians alike can wax eloquent about "the quest for knowledge" as if it were somehow exempt from the pain associated with more prosaic forms of work. No one ever got a graduate degree, whether masters or doctorate, on forty-hour work weeks! The frontiers of knowledge take pioneering sweat. And like the settlers who carved out new lives for themselves from the Australian bush or the American prairie, the pain often seems endless and the frustration without surcease. The work goes on. And the questions persist to defy the latest "answers." Will there ever be a cure for cancer? What about AIDS? Is our very existence intelligible?

This perennial search is "a heavy burden God has laid on men" (1:13b). It is not that study is a drag because it can wear us out physically, even though it can and often does. Neither is study wearisome because the world and its problems are unintelligible in their very nature, even if it sometimes can seem that way. The real reason is that God has placed a burden on us! He has imposed a set of limitations upon us that were not always there. We are subject to a kind of discipline that keeps us down, that keeps us, in other words, from ever being so swimmingly successful that we can bathe in the conceit that we are gods, with exhaustive knowledge and monolithic control over our lives under the sun. Qoheleth is alluding here, of course, to the curse that was, and remains, a consequence of man's fall into sin (Gen. 3:17-19). The whole creation is subject to this judicial consequence of man's ethical rebellion against God (Rom. 8:20). In this context, the focus is on the unremitting quest for answers to the meaning of life. This is neither merely a circumstance of human psychology nor simply a cultural or sociological phenomenon. It is a thirst, an inner compulsion, a facet of human nature implanted by God. It aches for answers and cries out for relief—and, when it limits itself to an under-the-sun outlook, it comes up empty again and again. The point is that any search for meaning apart from God and his revealed will is bound to be frustrating—"a chasing after the wind" (1:14)—because it has the wrong starting point.

The difficulty is compounded because some problems are incapable of resolution. In our scientific age, we expect answers. We expect the doctors to heal our diseases: we expect engineers to build bigger and better bridges and aircraft. The public face of modern scholarship is one of limitless answers to life's practical problems . . . in time and with the right funding! The reality is quite different. Where it matters—in human behavior, individual and social— the darkness remains and even deepens. And the wise men go around and around, as they have for centuries, looking in vain for answers under the sun. What is "twisted" still "cannot be straightened" (1:15).

Knowledge, Once Attained, Fails (1:16-18)

A little knowledge may be a dangerous thing, but a lot of it can sometimes be downright depressing. How many times have you wished you knew what was going to happen? Let's suppose you could see the future. Would it solve your present fears? It would, of course, remove uncertainty. But, strange as it may seem, uncertainty is not the greatest of our difficulties in life. A far greater problem is that of *controlling our destiny*. That is the true root of our concern with the future and its uncertainties.

Even an ability to predict the future would actually be a dubious asset. Why? Because it could not guarantee any capacity to channel that future to our welfare. A simple example of this would be a situation in which you are tied to a railroad track knowing that the 9:30 Express will be on time and you can do nothing about it! A great deal of scholarship—and all of occult practices and witch-craft—attempts to make up this kind of deficiency and exercise a tangible control over events. Scientific models are constructed in such a way as to anticipate likely future scenarios and thus, scientists hope, exercise a measure of control over contingencies as they arise. Bridges are engineered. Diplomacy is shaped. Plans are drawn. Armies are deployed. Such models or predictions often represent considerable wisdom. They may actually influence future actions. But they cannot be said to constitute *sovereignty* over imminent events in any ultimate and therefore absolutely sure sense. Rudyard Kipling's somber and prophetic imperialist hymn, "Recessional," expresses something of that endemic inadequacy of man's best laid plans. Spoken to the British Empire at its magnificent apogee, Kipling's words stand as both warning and epitaph for all the arrogance of godless power.

> Far-called, our navies melt away;
>   On dune and headland sinks the fire:
> Lo, all our pomp of yesterday
>   Is one with Nineveh and Tyre!
> Judge of the nations, spare us yet,
> Lest we forget—lest we forget![3]

If, then, we have no real control over eventualities, the mere knowledge of what was about to happen could be not an enlightening but a potentially devastating burden. More than a mere foreboding of a future threat, it would be painful awareness of things certain to come, without the amelioration of some power to influence or change them in any happier direction. As it is, our lives are frequently punctuated by clear knowledge of future experiences—some good, some not so good. Terminal illness can bring the numbering of our days to a poignant preciseness. We feel the trials and tribulations all the more keenly when they are anticipated. And while, with God's grace, these may occasion spiritual victories of the most exalted sweetness, without doubt these are the deep waters through which the soul must pass. Knowing our future troubles, especially, is never a thrill. To know them *all* might seem little better than a species of hell.

Qoheleth looks at his personal experience. He took his thinking very seriously. He was a wise man. And precisely because of that, he saw the realities. Ignorance is a kind of bliss, after all, for "with much wisdom, comes much sorrow; the more knowledge, the more grief" (1:8). It would be a great mistake to see this as a commendation of ignorance, however. The frying pan may be cooler than a fire, but it is not the context for a happy and fulfilling life! There is a German proverb that sums it up with untranslatable pathos: *"Viel Wissen macht Kopfweh,"* meaning, "Much knowledge gives one a headache."[4] In a fallen and imperfect world, pain snaps at the heels of our best endeavors. But to labor in the belief that we shall solve the problem of the meaning of life, outside of a personal trust in God and a feeding upon his Word, is to institutionalize futility and clothe our life with the frustrating reality that we may be always learning but never seem able to come to the knowledge of the truth (II Tim. 3:7).

Pleasure Palls (2:1-11)

If the failure of knowledge represents the bankruptcy of rationalism, then to turn to pleasure as a solution is to dip into the well of irrationalism. When the books don't give the answers, it's time to pass the bottle! "I thought in my heart," says Qoheleth, " 'Come now, I will test you with pleasure to find out what is good'" (2:1). What many do just because they want to, Qoheleth turns into an experiment. Where knowledge fails, can fun succeed? Can the joys of sense and flesh give the lasting satisfaction that he—and we—crave with body and soul? Can hedonism—the indulgence of the senses—provide fulfillment and meaning?

Some people seem to think so. The *Gentleman's Quarterly* for June 1987, ran an article about the things a "gentleman" should do by age thirty. These included, among a list of 99 items, having sex 1,248 times with 19 partners. Commenting on this, Robert Ingram noted that the significant point is that this publication "not only advocates and endorses hedonism, but also speaks of it in terms of 'oughtness' or moral imperatives." It reveals, he adds, "an 'under the sun' ethical system where God is absent."[5]

This was the philosophy of the Cyrenaics, a fifth-century-B.C. school of Greek philosophers, who, along with another, more famous school, the Epicureans, held that religion (fear of future punishment for sin) was a burden that ruined the enjoyment of this present life. The Cyrenaics advocated freedom to bathe in the pleasures of the senses, with relatively little regard to the consequences. Gordon Clark wryly records the parody of the Cyrenaic motto: "Eat, drink and be merry, for tomorrow we shall have gout, cirrhosis of the liver and delirium tremens."[6] For them, real pleasure was the pleasure *of the moment* – the experience of the pleasurable act.

The Epicureans were more moderate. For them, the known evil consequences of sensual pleasures operated as a limiting factor in defining the nature of true pleasure. They principally emphasized the pleasures of the intellect and, being less self-destructive than the Cyrenaics, survived as an important school for several centuries. The apostle Paul encountered some of them on Mars Hill in Athens (Acts 17:18).[7]

We naturally identify hedonism with the excesses of sensualism – of endless partying and having a "good time" – and think of it as a mere frivolity gone to seed. But it is more than that. It is, as we have seen, a strand of philosophy with a most venerable lineage. As such, it is far more than an excuse or a rationalization for the fun time! It is a well-marked trail along which many generations have sought true meaning in life. It is this, I believe, that Qoheleth gave himself to investigate. He did not experiment with gross sin. He simply analyzed some of the apparently otherwise harmless, or ostensibly productive, ways in which people amuse themselves.

Let's Have a Party! (2:2-3)

Fun and frolic are the obvious avenues of hedonistic expression. Have you ever been at a party and laughed so much that your facial muscles almost cramped up! Even when the jokes kept flowing, but didn't seem funny anymore, you began to feel that your smile was becoming painfully fixed on your face? Fun – even good clean fun—can pall after a while. Qoheleth is referring to this kind of "laughter" (2:2a [Heb., *sehoq*]; cf. Prov. 10:23; Eccles. 10:19), fine for light relief, as yet another blind alley in the quest for meaning.

Furthermore, "pleasure" (2:2b [Heb., *simha*])—the thoughtful pleasure that enjoys good things—secures no lasting satisfaction. The gourmet palate, the connoisseur of paintings and sculpture, the exhilaration of the raconteur's wit . . . accomplish what? "The implication of the rhetorical question is obvious," observes Michael Eaton, "all pleasures, high-brow and low-brow alike, fail to meet the needs of the man whose horizon remains 'under the sun.'"[8] For all that, Qoheleth pressed on in his investigation. Lubricated by the genteel enjoyment of the fruit of the vine, he engaged in the mental exercise of "embracing folly"—giving his mind to the widest range of "what was worthwhile for men to do under heaven during the few days of their lives" (2:3).[9] He drew deeply from the well of fun—but came up empty.

Cultured Excess (2:4-11)

Creativity and self-expression may also be the focus of hedonistic excess. And what of these deeper, seemingly more durable pleasures? Categories like creativity and self-expression are assumed ipso facto to be a cut above a night out with the boys. If the latter dissolves into a hazy memory of happy camaraderie or the oblivion of a hangover, the former has the virtue of ostensibly enhancing the common cultural heritage of humanity. Creativity has to it an aura of public service. Any potential for self-indulgence can be balanced by a countervailing motive of altruism and a sense of lasting contribution to the common good. And there surely is a legitimate joy in works of creative self-expression. Art galleries, museums, ruined castles, magnificent palaces, great literature, stamp collections, well-tended gardens, and the whole vast mosaic of human cultural achievement enhance the quality and enjoyment of life. Even a "folly"—one of these whimsical and, from a strictly utilitarian viewpoint, useless buildings put up by some mad, or simply humorous, landowner[10]—survives to amuse the tourists of later times.

But do these activities, laudable in themselves, constitute meaning in any ultimate sense, or are they just another overestimated avenue of otherwise impressive and praiseworthy human accomplishment? Qoheleth, as Solomon *redivivus*, muses about the projects of a great king (2:4-10). Houses, vineyards, gardens, parks, reservoirs, slaves, wealth, a harem—all the marks of a cultured and opulent Oriental monarch were developed to the full. But had even these highest realizations of human potential and aspiration resolved the real questions? Qoheleth thinks not. "In all this," he says, "my wisdom stayed with me" (2:9). He had kept a sense of reality and proportion. His things of beauty did not strike him as a joy *forever.* "To call such things eternal is no more than rhetoric, and nothing perishable will satisfy him."[11] It was just sweat, "a chasing after the wind; nothing was gained under the sun" (2:11). Even the most sophisticated of pleasures offers only an illusory escape from the prison of secularism. Aestheticism, sensualism, and creativitism end within themselves. What you see is what you get! The paths of such glory lead but inwardly—and turn full circle upon themselves.

Death Comes to Us All (2:12-16)

Death is the wall that under-the-sun secularism cannot climb. Even the remembrance of those who have died perishes with those who knew them personally. Beethoven may be said to live on in his music, but the truth is that we know the music, not the man. The names and acts of the famous and notorious remain in the written records and the oral traditions of mankind. But outside of these selective and even arbitrary memorials, the good and the bad, the foolish and the wise, perish into anonymity (2:15-16). Dust they were and to dust they returned! True, says Qoheleth, wisdom is better than folly, even under the sun. Even the "children of Adam" have a kind of wisdom—at least they have eyes in their heads (2:12-14)! But what can it mean, if death is all there is?

"I hated life" (2:17-23)

The answer is brutally simple: If death is where it all ends, it makes nonsense of the journey. Life is little different from the pirate's walk down the plank. You call that meaning? Death laughs at all the moments of our lives. It curses life and casts its shadow over our work. We toil away in order to sustain a life for its extinction! Where is the sense in that! And where is there any comfort, when I am annihilated into atomized oblivion, in the fruit of my labors falling to another? There is no satisfaction for those who have ceased to exist. Therefore, says Qoheleth, "I hated life" (2:17). In the under-the-sun scheme of things, this is the depressing conclusion of intelligent reflection. How many cling to life, only because they fear death more? The *objects* of our toil become repulsive (2:18). The *future inheritors* of the fruit of that work become a source of frustration (2:19). The very *experience* of toil blights the days and nights (2:23). All these are meaningless, say Qoheleth. An aching emptiness claws at the heart. The last resting place of the secular mind is the aching anticlimax of absolute nonbeing.

Answers to Pessimism (2:24-26)

Is life itself just a dead end? Are all our experiences along the way no more than polishing brass on a sinking ship? If, in the words of the rock group, The Grateful Dead, we are "going to hell in a bucket," shouldn't we be "enjoying the ride on the way"? Should we not just say, "Let us eat and drink, for tomorrow we die"? (I Cor. 15:32).

Qoheleth gives three answers to these questions, and each one heralds a radical change of tone from all that he has hitherto been saying.

Enjoy Life! (2:24a)

"A man can do nothing better" is a recurring theme in Ecclesiastes (2:24; 3:12, 22; 8:15). It affirms that what has become a burden ought to be a great joy! Qoheleth starts here with something everyone can understand: metaphysics and bad cooking aside, eating and drinking can be a joy. So, he quietly suggests, why take a jaundiced view of these things? Why not receive them for what they are? Why not accept them as blessings? After all, life itself is a marvelous thing. Does it not look to you as something designed to be good and to do good? He does not mention it, but did he intend to remind his readers that God had made all things good (Gen. 2:9)? Had God not repeatedly spoken of his provision of material comfort and prosperity as a blessing? He "richly provides us with everything for our enjoyment" (I Tim. 6:17). "For everything God created is good, and nothing is to be rejected if it is received with thanksgiving" (I Tim. 4:4). God has made a lavish provision for us: "wine that gladdens the heart of man, oil to make his face shine, and bread that sustains his heart" (Ps. 104:15). The point of contact with his skeptical readers—more than that, the *schwerpunkt*, the point of breakthrough—is the fundamental fact that we respond to good things with enjoyment. We may therefore argue from that positive provision and pleasurable experience to the meaning and purpose of these things. Life is meant to be satisfying!

Life Is a Gift! (2:24b-25)

From experience, Qoheleth turns to faith—and the ultimate reality that interprets our experience correctly: "This too, I see, is from the hand of God, for without him, who can eat or find enjoyment?" Receiving life as a gift is impossible without receiving the Giver. This is the condition of true fulfillment, according to Qoheleth. The reasonableness of his argument rests on the incontrovertible awareness of meaninglessness in the under-the-sun world view. It is a matter of "no God, no goal." Mind you, only a very few will out-and-out admit that. The secular-materialist hangs on with grim determination to the notion that he really is going somewhere. But we must insist, against his claims: Does this creation not witness to the reality of the God who made it and reveals himself in the Bible (Ps. 19:1-6; Rom. 1:18-20)? Is life not a gift? The language with which we normally describe the accomplished child and the creative craftsman expresses the theological truth undergirding our very existence. We call them *gifted* individuals. In our hearts and consciences we know that life is a gift and that there is a Giver.

Receive the Joy! (2:26)

God gives true wisdom and joy to those who please him. This answers a very important question that is a stumbling block to many. On what basis does God apportion his blessings? After all, there are wide disparities in human experience and the demarcation line is not a simple one between the rich and the poor. Discontent and despair cut through both groups. There is no need to resort to the stereotypes of "humble poor" and "stinking rich" to explain this. God does not make all his believers rich according to the conventional materialistic standards of the day. What is significant is that he *provides* and *transforms*, so that he is glorified in the praise of his people—which includes every aspect of renewed lives.

There is in this a very positive message for those who feel the icy hand of hopelessness closing in on their lives: Through a living faith in God, there is joy in the simplest and the most complex of life's experiences. Both the eternal love of God that secures that new life and the newborn faith with which the new believer comes into a saved relationship with God center in the cross. Jesus Christ, the only mediator between God and man, atoned for all the sins of all his people, as their substitute. In his sufferings and death, he despised the shame and satisfied the perfect justice of God. God's love secured the satisfaction of his own justice in sending his Son to die for other people's sins. And the pivotal point for men and women is, therefore, how we respond to Jesus Christ. He calls us to believe on the Lord Jesus Christ that we might be saved (see I Tim. 2:5; Matt. 1:21; I Cor. 15:3; John 3:16).

Qoheleth concludes his challenge with a solemn warning. To him who rejects his overtures of grace ("the sinner") there can only be a darkening prospect. In an anticipation of our Lord's parable about the rich fool (Luke 12:13-21) and other teachings of the New Testament (Matt. 5:5; Luke 19:24; I Cor. 3:21; II Cor. 6:10), Qoheleth serves God's notice about his judgments upon the under-the-sun lifestyle. The fruits of their labors will not be enjoyed by them but will benefit the lives of God's people. Referring to this loss of the blessing that could be theirs, he remarks (and we can almost hear his sorrowful sigh), "This too is meaningless, a chasing after the wind!" (2:26).

Questions for Discussion

1. Why did the writer find "knowledge" (rationalism) to be, in itself "meaningless, chasing after the wind" (1:12-18)? What light do Genesis 3:17-19 and Romans 8:20 shed on these difficulties?

2. What do verses 16-18 tell us about the effectiveness of knowledge once it is attained? Does knowledge really help us *control our destiny?* Discuss the failure of rationalism as an outlook on life.

3. Why is "fun and frolic" (hedonism) a dead-end in the search for meaning (2:2-3)? Discuss the role of creativity and self-expression (2:4-11). Are "things of beauty" a "joy forever"?

4. What does Qoheleth say about death (2:12-16)?

5. Why does the writer say "I hated life" (2:17-23)?

6. What are the Lord's answers to this pessimism (2:24-26)? How ought life to be lived (cf. I Tim. 4:4; 6:17; Ps. 104:15; Luke 12:13-21)?

3
WHO'S IN CHARGE?
Please Read Ecclesiastes 3:1-22

> There is a time for everything,
> and a season for every activity under heaven:
> a time to be born and a time to die,
> a time to plant and a time to uproot,
> a time to kill and a time to heal. . . .
>
> Ecclesiastes 3:1-3

Time magazine recently used a catchy and effective TV advertisement drawn from Ecclesiastes 3:1-8. A song, illustrated by suitable and beautiful film clips, told us that there is "a time to be born and a time to die . . . a time to weep and a time to laugh" and so forth. The words "Turn, turn, turn" were insinuated between the couplets as a sort of back-up accompaniment to remind of the real purpose of the exercise. And what was the message? Simply that *Time* will keep us abreast of the times. The events of human life as they unfold in all their variety will be reported to us as they happen. We subscribe, then we "turn, turn, turn" the pages and the births, deaths, laughs, and cries will tumble out in profusion to shed their light upon our way. *Time* will make sense of a myriad of happenings, by editorial selection of the news they deem significant. History will, in this way, be decanted from the great vat of otherwise undifferentiated eventuality. Meaning—insofar as "newsak" gets below the surface—will be drawn from the well of meaningless contingent factuality! And we will feel informed!

Qoheleth, however, had something different in mind in writing Ecclesiastes 3. As he saw it, the problem with human events is not merely one of practical journalism—how to select the news to be published. It is not a sorting, still less a packaging problem. It is, rather, how we are to understand the facts themselves. Do they *just happen*? Are they related or unrelated? Can they be connected meaningfully because they are meaningful in themselves? Or is meaning merely what the human mind imposes on intrinsically amorphous facts? Again, are the facts essentially meaningless and are we therefore alone, to be buffeted about by ultimate unpredictability on every hand, our only comfort being that one day Ph.D. candidates will gain degrees for inventive theorizing about its possible significance?

These are not rarified questions. They are about ultimate realities that touch our lives every day. Events in the world around us always seem much bigger than we are. For example, everybody talks about the weather a great deal. Why? Because weather can so easily alter our plans. The elements expose how puny we are, how tenuous our control of our lives really is. Many other circumstances beyond our control arise from time to time. "The best laid plans of mice and men," said Scots poet Robert Burns, "gang aft agley"—and we don't need a translation to catch the meaning!

It is very possible to be afraid and to feel very alone in such a world. Most powerful of all, personal tragedies always bid to crush the person who has no core conviction as to the meaning and purpose of the flow of history and no secure sense of who he is. Even the anticipation of future horrors that may never come has sent some fearful soul into a tailspin of inconsolable despair.

Nonetheless, the survivors are in the majority. There is a steely determination in the resolution of the defiantly godless to live out their under-the-sun lives as best they can, given the uninviting end to which their existence, by their own way of it, must come. At one end of the spectrum of self-reliance we have the trembling resignation of those who see a less-than-palatable future but have decided to get on with the job anyway. But at the other extreme is the fervent humanism of a man like the poet W. E. Henley, who throws down his gauntlet before the claims of God and centers all meaning in autonomous man.

In the fell clutch of circumstance,
    I have not winced nor cried aloud:
Under the bludgeonings of chance
    My head is bloody but unbowed.

It matters not how straight the gate,
    How charged with punishments the scroll.
I am the master of my fate,
    I am the captain of my soul.[1]

Henley really was speaking for the under-the-sun perspective. A
more cautious and less brutally analytical person will just cross his
fingers, hope for the best, and put aside disquieting thoughts about
ultimate questions. But he nevertheless lives out Henley's creed in
practice, even if he would balk at confessing it as his faith. And as
long as the sun shines and the wine is good, so to speak, he enjoys
being the master of his fate and the captain of his soul. All anti-
supernaturalism has no option but to live that way. Cracks begin
to show when adversity strikes. Then a defiance that rests, in fact,
on a foundation no more substantial than the words themselves
crumbles to a litany of aching emptiness and fearful isolation:
"Why did this happen to me? What does it all mean? I can't understand it. What will I do now? I don't know if I can go on . . ." These
are the kinds of questions and doubts to which the passage under
study directs an answer.

There Is a Time for Everything (3:1-8)
Merely to state that "there is a time for everything" (3:1) is to imply
purpose and direction, to assert the controlling power of an intelligent providence, to declare that God is on the throne.

Qoheleth is certainly not saying that it so happens that events
occur at different times. That would be a statement of the obvious.
Neither is he saying that there is a kind of cyclical inevitability to
the flow of time. He is not dolefully observing that life goes on according to some rhythm of the spheres. And he is not talking
about some human responsibility to live in an ordered and timely
way, as if it is in our hands to make something of an otherwise inherently purposeless existence.

Qoheleth's point is the precise opposite of these points of view. God, he says, "has made everything beautiful in its time" (3:11). The sovereignty of God transcends the whole life of humanity in the world. In other words, whatever human agency may be involved in all the activities recorded in Ecclesiastes 3:2-8, these are in fact the acts of God, in which he unfolds his hitherto secret will for our lives. Even the most free actions of men take place within the all-encompassing embrace of God's absolute sovereignty. Scripture applies this principle to the most concrete and dire circumstances. "My *times* are in your hands" prays the psalmist; "deliver me from my enemies and those who pursue me" (Ps. 31:15). God declares: "I choose *the appointed time*; it is I who judge uprightly. When the earth and all its people quake, it is I who hold its pillars firm" (Ps. 75:2). God "will arise and have compassion on Zion, for it is *time* to show favor to her; *the appointed time* has come" (Ps. 102:13). The great turning point of history – the cross of Jesus Christ – is spoken of in similar terms. It was said of Jesus in his earlier ministry that no one could lay a hand on him, "because his *time* had not yet come" (John 7:30). But on the night he was betrayed by Judas Iscariot, our Lord said of himself: "Father, *the time* has come. Glorify your Son, that your Son may glorify you" (John 17:1). Far from being at the mercy of random eventualities, we await the unfolding of "God's set purpose and foreknowledge" (Acts 2:23).

Think, then, of the variegated facets of life. From birth and death (3:2), Qoheleth ranges across the life experiences of ordinary people, demonstrating to reflective minds that the events that shape our lives are much larger than any pretentions we might have to exercise control over them. Martin Luther, with characteristic bluntness, gets to the heart of the matter.

> All this is directed against the free will of man, and against all human purposes and fancies, but especially against the notion that it is in our power to determine seasons, and hours, and persons, and measures and place; that we can settle how the affairs of this world shall go, how its great potentates shall rise and fall, how joy and sadness, building up and pulling down, war and peace, shall succeed and take the place of each other, how they shall begin and end: it is to impress on us the

fact that ere the hour arrives it is wasted effort for men to
think and their proposals are useless and vain: in fine, we are
taught that nothing comes to pass before the hour fixed for it
by God.[2]

Qoheleth's poetic couplets amass an argument in support of this
thesis. Twenty-five centuries on, we have little difficulty identifying
with his evocation of the universal human condition: birth and
death, planting and uprooting, killing and healing, tearing down
and building up, weeping and laughing, mourning and dancing,
scattering and gathering stones, embracing and refraining from
embracing, searching and giving up, keeping and throwing away,
tearing and mending, keeping silent and speaking out, loving and
hating, waging war and making peace; these touch us, uplift us,
buffet us, exhilarate us, disappoint us, and, sometimes, devastate
us. And, for the most part, they happen *to* us. From outside of us,
these forces conspire to lead us by the nose, often against the current of our fondest aspirations and our well-laid plans!

We most naturally internalize these themes and mesh them with
our personal individual experience. But as John Donne said, no
man is an island. Even the most personal of events—birth and
death—cannot be locked up into the individual who is born or
who dies. A birth is a powerful event in the life of a mother, of
other family members, of physicians and nurses, and involves a
myriad of other people, all before the baby has the cognitive equip-
ment to reflect on its own existence. An intricate web of relationships forms the matrix of all life experiences. Qoheleth is not simply
concerned with the thought life of the individual; he is speaking to
folk who had a very deep people-consciousness. Israel was a nation
imbued with a profound sense of corporate identity. They were
God's people—a fact that rendered their increasing under-the-sun
secularization an intensely puzzling and distressing phenomenon.
That the covenant people of a loving Father-God should need to
be challenged about this problem speaks volumes about the dis-
tance they had fallen.

The text itself gives more than a hint of a wider, corporate dimension. The most obvious clue, to modern readers, is in the curi-
ous words, There is "a time to scatter stones and a time to gather

them" (3:5a). What can this mean? Whatever it is, it would not appear to be any immediately apparent normal activity of people today. The answer is to be found by comparing Scripture with Scripture. When Jesus prophesied the destruction of the temple in Jerusalem, he said: "Do you see all these great buildings? . . . Not one stone here will be left on another; every one will be thrown down" (Mark 13:2). The scattering of stones represents the judgment of God; the obliteration of the temple and its worship signaled the fact that it had ceased to be the true house of God. It was standard practice in Old Testament times for conquering armies both to scatter stones on their enemies fields to make them unproductive (II Kings 3:19, 25; Isa. 5:2) and to gather stones for the purpose of preparing the highway for the advance of the victorious soldiers (Isa. 62:10).[3]

This suggests that God has given Qoheleth a word for the *whole* people of God and not just for individuals in their private lives. Who does this scattering and gathering of stones in due time? God does it, through whoever his agents may be, and he does it in terms of his righteous discipline of his erring people. A closer look at the other categories mentioned unveils that same perspective. God is speaking to his people so that they, his church, may understand both their afflictions and their times of blessing as falling under the sovereignty and faithfulness of the living God. Herbert Leupold writes, "There is a periodicity about the things that happen to the Zion of God that helps us to understand her state and to know how far the hand of God is involved in what transpires."[4]

Planting and uprooting (3:2b) relate to the history of Israel's deliverance from Egypt (Pss. 44:2; 80:8, 12); killing and healing (2:3a) have more than an echo in divine judgment and redemption (Deut. 32:39; Hos. 6:11); and love and hatred toward God's people (2:8a) have arisen according to the purposes of God (cf. Ps. 105:25; Exod. 13:3). In every case, including birth and death, the language used has both an individual and a corporate application. The words of Scripture are used with great precision. When with careful study we are able to make the connections with the overall flow of the biblical message, we can discern not only the immediate and personal thrust of the Word of God, but the eschatological and corporate dimension that opens up the meaning of the temporal and the eternal destiny of the people of God. Qoheleth speaks to the church as a whole as well as to the individual; he speaks to the "now" of day-to-day life and also to the "not yet" of God's purposes for his church in the world. He interprets past, present, and future and says to all who have ears to hear, There is true meaning both in what is happening to you now and in what is yet to take place. God has set the times and the seasons for everything under heaven. So, if we are tempted to view events and experiences in exclusively secular, under-the-sun terms, Qoheleth reminds us that, in fact, these same events and experiences take place under *heaven* — and heaven is the throne of the sovereign God, who makes everything "beautiful in its time" (3:11a).

Eternity in People's Hearts (3:9-11)

In interpreting the "time for everything" passage (3:1-8), we have anticipated what follows. Those eight verses never mention God and do not attempt to define their relevance to the overall theme of Ecclesiastes. But nothing in the Bible just hangs there in isolation from the rest of Scripture. On the surface there may be an enigmatic quality to the passage, but, as we have seen, the very words that are used shed light on its deeper meaning. We do not, however, have long to wait for an explicit interpretation. And it is introduced with a very practical and searching question: "What does the worker gain from his toil?" (3:9).

This is a repeat of the first question Qoheleth ever asked (1:3). He is a shrewd judge of human nature. When you tell someone who doesn't share your faith that God is in control of everything, how do they often react? Don't they say, "Well, if that's so, where's the sense in us doing anything at all?" They see a tension between God's sovereignty, as you see it, and human freedom, as they see it. This is a legitimate question. After all, there is so much evidence that people do what they want, often with frightening consequences, that it can seem very strange special pleading to say that all of this has fallen out according to God's plan from before the creation of the world. Even an atheist would acknowledge that believing God is in control could be a great comfort to someone sinking in a sea of troubles. His problem is that he just doesn't believe it, so it offers him no comfort. He just sees the apparent tension. And he sees it as a contradiction of simple logic. If God exists and is in control, then why bother about anything?

Well, says Qoheleth, let's talk about the human condition (3:10-11). He returns to the thought of 1:13, where he spoke of the burden God had placed upon man, and gives further explanation. He agrees that man has a burden. It is not just that he needs to know about his world and has an insatiable appetite for largely futile study (1:13-18). No! He has an even deeper need. He needs to know why his toil—indeed, his whole life—can have some profit to it in a world beyond his personal control. The problem for the under-the-sun generation is that the idea that there is a God who orders all their "times" and "seasons" is a more perturbing threat to their self-image as the new age autonomous humanity than the concept that they are alone in a dying universe. Against such practical atheism, Qoheleth offers three answers.

Everything Is Beautiful (3:11a)

God "has made everything beautiful in its time" (3:11a). Why go on in self-destructive skepticism? "Care and toil begin, when faith and prayer cease; but out of care and toil we rise again to faith and prayer."[5] The eye of faith sees the beauty in God's ordering of the times. The key to this perception is in the redemptive purposes of God for his people. All those aspects of life for which there is a time are seen in relation to the glory of the God who is saving his world, an inch at a time, from the institutionalized meaninglessness of satanic delusion and human emptiness. The believing church sees the heavenly symmetry of God's mighty acts in history, though invariably through the retrospective illumination of the Spirit and the Word in the arena of his faithful reflection on the signs of the times. For every believer, the gracious purposes of the Lord shine through the darkest passages of these times and, far from being a source of gloom, these become a fount of encouragement and joy in the Lord. There is a grand design. The evidence is there. Look up and see!

Eternity Within (3:11b)

God "has also set eternity in the hearts of men" (3:11b). An awareness of creaturehood carries with it a sense of the reality of the Creator (Rom. 1:20; cf. Ps. 90:1-5; Eccles. 12:7). This is the basis of the ache that men and women feel for something more enduring than this life. Our hearts, said Augustine, are restless till they find their rest in the Lord.[6] The suppression of this consciousness of God is at the core of sin and estrangement from God.

This Unfathomable Life (3:11c)

We "cannot fathom what God has done from beginning to end" (3:11c). Even though there is eternity in our hearts, we cannot fully grasp the meaning of things. Indeed, we even resist the pull of eternity and spiritual things. We look in the opposite direction for satisfaction. We imagine that secular knowledge and carnal pleasure will answer our deepest needs. And it is here that the burden is felt most painfully. The problem of meaning has its only answer in heaven, from the mouth of God. But lost humanity leaves no stone unturned under the sun! We look for answers in the wrong places. How desperately we need to be found by the one whom we do not seek (Isa. 65:1)!

The Gifts of God (3:12-15)

Overarching the human condition, however, is God's gracious provision (3:12-15). Quiet passion suffuses Qoheleth's words. With two "I know . . ." statements, he affirms his most deeply held conclusions.

The Gift of God (3:12-13)

Life is both a privilege and a pleasure for the friends of God. Complaining that God's sovereign control over everything renders our efforts meaningless is actually a veiled rationalization of practical atheism. The real argument behind such cavils is this: I believe I am free and autonomous and cannot see that there is any predestinating power in control of my actions. Qoheleth's point is that anyone who truly believes and trusts in God joyfully embraces the assurance that God is in charge of the times and seasons and on that basis receives the gifts of his loving and bountiful provision for his believing people. The children of God exult in the Lord who has cattle on a thousand hills and who is the suzerain of the created universe (Pss. 50:10; 24:1). The pursuit of God-centered and God-honoring happiness, enjoyment of good food and drink, a zeal for doing good to all men, and satisfaction in one's work – all these are legitimate goals for God's people. They are his gifts. And therefore they are our calling. The Christian is not called to live out life as a subsistence-survivalist in a Kafkaesque nightmare of a world. He is called, even in the "valley of the shadow of death" (which this world always will be until the Lord returns), to enjoy a plentiful table and the goodness and love of his Lord all the days of his life (Ps. 23:5-6).

Our True Security (3:14-15)
The works of God "endure forever" (3:14a). They are complete and we can neither add to nor subtract from their ultimate perfection. Seeing how awesome his works are, "men will revere him" (3:14b). The practical fruit of God's sovereignty will be a worshiping people, exulting in the security of their Savior-God. And where some have to pass through the waters of persecution, there is the assurance that "God will call the past to account" (3:15). The everlasting arms surround the people of God wherever they may be (Ps. 139).

The Tests of Life (3:16-22)
If bad experiences are sometimes blessings in disguise, they sure can be very well disguised! Injustice and oppression scream out for redress and always persist much longer than human patience considers acceptable. There is, in our impatience, an implicit outrage against the tardiness of God to exercise what we regard as being his proper justice. It does not come naturally to us to consider that maybe – just maybe – some of the disasters and injustices were subserving the righteous purposes of God. The truth is, however, that we all want heaven now and as cheaply as possible, so we find it difficult to take the long view. Real faith is required to rest in the Lord and wait patiently for him, accepting humbly that he is truthful when he says he is "not slow in keeping his promise, as

some understand slowness" (II Pet. 3:9; cf. vv. 8-13). And the reality, or otherwise, of that faith is tested by the rampant evil that some people inflict on other people.

Qoheleth saw the tragedy of oppression in his own time. The doctrine of the witches in Shakespeare's *Macbeth* was stamped on the portals of Israel's justice: "Fair is foul and foul is fair." "In the place of justice—wickedness was there" (3:16). When the law becomes lawless, hope vanishes like morning dew, and moral anarchy becomes the currency of daily life in a dog-eat-dog world. "Where is God when we need him?" is the harsh but compelling cry of desperate pragmatism.

A twofold answer slices through the self-serving complaint that God is not fair to let such things go on.

Judgment Ahead! (3:17)

"God will bring to judgment both the righteous and the wicked" (3:17). We are neither automata nor autonomous. God gave man a certain freedom to live his life and called him to personal faith and discipleship. The Word was revealed as the rule of faith and practice. But man was not a puppet. He was called to choose whom he would serve. His response, from Adam to the present, has been to assert his autonomy from God. Well, says Qoheleth, that response was allowed. The world is full of evil. The time will come for reckoning. It is appointed to man to die once and then to face judgment. There is a time for ultimate divine justice!

Testing Now! (3:18-22)

The course of life and history is an arena of testing. "As for men, God tests them so that they may see that they are like the animals" (3:18, cf. vv. 19ff.). It is fashionable today to portray man as no more than a highly evolved animal—Desmond Morris's famous "naked ape." Qoheleth's intention is to press the opposite point of view by showing that when man lives an under-the-sun, anti-God, anti-faith existence, he consigns himself by his own standards to a status and destiny no more significant than that of animals. They both die . . . and that is *it*. By that standard, who knows where the spirits of men and animals go (3:19-21)? Qoheleth is not saying that a person who denies that he is made in the image of God and who insists on a secular earthbound lifestyle *is* no better than an animal. He is saying that his under-the-sun faith inevitably defines his existence and destiny as no different in principle from that of the animals. All we could say for sure is that, like them, we die and return to dust. Man, "despite his riches, does not endure; he is like the beasts that perish" (Ps. 49:12). But is this the last word? No, says the psalmist, "This is the fate of those who trust in themselves, and of their followers, who approve of their sayings. . . . But God will redeem my soul from the grave; he will surely take me to himself" (Ps. 49:13, 15). From the perspective of a person's world view, the difference is this: As all animals are radical existentialists in that they live entirely for moment-by-moment survival and have no future beyond the expiration of life, so under-the-sun human beings turn their backs on their true nature as God's offspring, made to be his image bearers in the world, and commit themselves to this-world existentialism.

What waste! What eternal dereliction! What sad blasphemy! What unspeakable folly! To reject the eternal love of the Father-God! To deny the high calling of man to be the image of God and to enter into glory through a salvation bought with the blood of the incarnate Son of God! To choose meaninglessness against the destiny of fellowship with God! O, take the way of life and meaning, pleads Qoheleth. Receive the gift of God!

There is, therefore, "nothing better for a man than to enjoy his work, because that is his lot" (3:22). You are "not the master of the future: therefore . . . rejoice in the present."[7] God has given the present to be enjoyed as it affords God-honoring opportunities to do so. The future must be the subject of a rising personal trust in the Lord, who is ordering our lives and calling us to be his men and women in the midst of a world that so profoundly needs his saving grace.

Questions for Discussion

1. Does everything "just happen". . . by chance? Review the fourteen pairs of events in 3:2-8.

2. What does this say about our "times" (see Pss. 31:15; 75:2; 102:13)?

Notice how Jesus' "times" were ordered in John 7:30; 17:1; Acts 2:23. How does this connect with our lives?

3. Even if we believe that God orders our lives, what do we still sometimes feel about life (vv. 9-10)? In response to this impression, how would Qoheleth answer the following questions:

    a. What is the true nature of things (v. 11a)?
    b. What is the true nature of man (v. 11b)?
    c. Why do we get confused (v. 11c)?

What does this tell us about our attitude to life?

4. How are we to view life (vv. 12-15)? See Psalms 24:1 and 50:10 for the basis of this outlook. How does Psalm 23:5-6 picture the life of God's people?

5. If life is God's gift, why can it be so hard? Why does God let such bad things go on . . . and on? And what will he do (vv. 16-21)?

6. What does II Peter 3:8-13 tell us about how we respond to life (see 3:22)?

PART TWO
PROBLEMS

4
EMPTY LIVES
Please Read Ecclesiastes 4:1-16

And I declared that the dead,
who had already died,
are happier than the living,
who are still alive.
But better than both
is he who has not yet been,
who has not seen the evil
that is done under the sun.

Ecclesiastes 4:2-3

Growing up in wet and windy Scotland, I always looked forward to one of those oh-so-rare "heat waves" when a stationary ridge of high pressure would sit long enough over the country to send the temperature "soaring" into the mid-seventies (yes! that's a Scottish heat wave!) and allow us to plan rain-free picnics at the beach. Alas, every silver lining seems to have its cloud! During these still periods the mornings and sometimes the afternoons would be blighted by what Scots call "the haar"—a cold, clinging mist that many a time has ruined an outing and kept the sweaters on in the middle of July! The best of things can so easily be blighted by an unexpected turn. Disappointment can come like that summer mist and suck meaningfulness out of the best of projects. The clammy tentacles of emptiness insinuate themselves into the happiest of lives and create a hollow feeling that can crush a person's spirit and bring him to despair. Qoheleth turns to a problem that threatens the most normal and tranquil of lives—the emptiness of earthly values in the context of particular, perennial, and potentially threatening social problems. He begins here to expound his main argument.

41

In the first three chapters, he sets the scene by surveying the general contours of our human predicament and the concomitant issues with which we must grapple in order to make sense and success of our lives. He spoke of the spiritual bankruptcy of secular, under-the-sun living (1:1-2:23). By way of contrast, he pointed briefly to the alternative, the life of faith in God (2:24-26). Finally, he argued for the certainties of God's providence and final judgment, urging, by implication, the necessity of receiving and enjoying life as the gift of God (3:1-22).

The next seven chapters (4:1-10:20) flesh out this thesis by highlighting particular problems and pointing to the Lord's answers. The recurring twin themes are, on the one hand, the utter emptiness of worldly values and, on the other hand, the meaning and joy that is to be found exclusively in a living faith relationship to God.

Ecclesiastes 4 isolates the practical problem of what we today might call "the rat race." Every generation tends, in its superior, narcissistic way, to think of its own situation as unique. And, of course, it is true that each age has its own character with new problems calling for fresh answers. We do not readily think of first millennium B.C. society as fitting the image conjured up by the term "rat race." Nevertheless, there were indeed analogous, if not exactly identical, pressures on the people of those distant centuries. When we filter out the hard core of their problems from their specific manifestation in the context of that day, we find that they touch our own lives in a very close and affecting way. Qoheleth takes the widest view of this phenomenon, touching down on major representative features that combine to erode the meaningfulness of people's lives. He begins with some grim observations about oppression and injustice, especially with reference to its devastating effect on those who suffer its depredations (4:1-3), and he ends with a somber assessment of the position of those most likely perpetrators of oppression—kings, who for all their power and fame, often live lonely lives, after which their memory recedes into a execrated past (4:13-16).

The Tears of the Oppressed (4:1-3)

"A sinful world," said Charles Bridges, "is a world of selfishness."[1] The world is full of oppressive governments, exploitative businesses and, not least, people who simply take advantage of others. The Robin Hood type of legend is so powerfully appealing precisely because of the generally oppressive climate of human societies. For many, if not most, people from the past to the present, freedom extends little further than the door of the soul. The Swiss-based organization, Christian Solidarity International — a society that is committed to supporting Christians under persecution from the state throughout the world with a ministry of prayer, public awareness, and legal representation — recently listed no fewer than fifty-seven countries in the world where governments harass or proscribe faithful Christian witness. These include states of all political colors and encompass virtually all of Asia, half of Africa, Eastern Europe, and a number of countries in Latin America.[2] And in the "Free World," the inundation of the courts with lawsuits and criminal prosecutions; the overcrowding of the prisons; and, the most poignantly, the roll of abused children, rape victims, the swindled, the maimed, and the murdered cry to heaven for justice in behalf of the prey of the oppressors.

God condemns such oppression in his Word in the strongest and most comprehensive terms. In modern language, the Scriptures roundly condemn all exploitation, whether by the state (Prov. 28:16), the wealthy (Amos 4:1), the law (Amos 5:12), the church (I Sam. 2:12-17; Matt. 23:23-24; cf. I Pet. 5:1-5), employers (Deut. 24:14), property agents (Mic. 2:2), bankers (Ezek. 22:12, 29), or businessmen (Hos. 12:7). And yet, there is so little concern for those who are lashed by the waves of cynical depredation. Qoheleth observes, "I saw the tears of the oppressed, and they have no comforter; power was on the side of their oppressors — and they have no comforter" (4:1b).

The psalmist pleaded, "Look to my right hand and see; no one is concerned for me. I have no refuge; no one cares for my life" (Ps. 142:4). The dying in the streets of Calcutta or the destitute in the barrios of Latin America might say the same today. This is the universal cry of the oppressed.

The ultimate experience of oppression was, of course, that of the Lord Jesus Christ himself. He was hated in spite of his perfect sinlessness — or because of it. Speaking of this hatred, he said, "But this is to fulfill what is written in their Law: 'They hated me without reason'" (John 15:25). The words quoted by the Lord are from Psalm 69:4—a passage that describes prophetically the experience of Christ at the hands of his detractors. "Scorn has broken my heart and left me helpless; I looked for sympathy, but there was none, for comforters, but I found none" (Ps. 69:20).

The Christian response to the cry of the oppressed is supposed to be precisely the opposite of this sort of treatment. We are, for example, to "remember those in prison as if [we] were their fellow prisoners" (Heb. 13:3). This flows from the central truth of the gospel, namely, that Jesus subjected himself to humiliation and suffering, including not only the unjust oppression of wicked men, but also the wholly just wrath of God against *our* sins. He did this to redeem us from sin by making atonement for sin as the substitute who bears that sin in the place of sinners—taking and satisfying the penalty due them. Part of that great complex of sin is a brutal lack of compassion. In the parable of the good Samaritan, Jesus vividly highlighted the callous indifference of the Levite, who when he spotted the victim of the Jericho Road muggers, preferred to pass by on the other side, not to get involved, and, needless to say, leave the compassion to somebody else—in that case to a despised (by Jews) Samaritan! Jesus' sufferings and death were the supreme act of compassion. He was despised and rejected by men, a man of sorrows and familiar with suffering. But when we hid, as it were, our faces from him (Isa. 53:3), he answered our hard hearts with steadfast love and sovereignly given and freely bestowed grace (Rom. 5:6). For this reason, the first evidence of having truly received Christ—the first fruit of the Holy Spirit's work of grace in our hearts—is a love for the Lord that overflows with compassion for others in their need. In the New Testament era, which means *right now*, some oppressed soul should be able to say, "I looked for sympathy . . . and I found Christ . . . in the compassionate love of his people!" Where there are Christians, compassion should flow like a mighty river.

A world full of oppression, assessed in purely secular terms, offers little or no hope of any redressing of the imbalances of injustice and lack of compassion. It presents a depressing canvas of unrelieved and largely irretrievable injustice and misery. And this may be said in spite of all the institutionalized compassion of secular society through wealth redistribution and social engineering programs. There is even evidence, as Herbert Schlossberg puts it, that "the source of the problem is in its putative solution."[3] That is to say these expressions of the secular "caring society" have been counterproductive and have actually exacerbated the problems they were designed to relieve. Be that as it may, it is small wonder in the face of present realities that thoughts of death as the great escape route begin to spring up in the minds of an increasing number of people. Qoheleth anticipates this—and even goes beyond it—in what has to be one of the most brutally frank expositions of the naked emptiness of the "hope" of the godless secularist. The dead are happier than the living, he says, but the unborn are better off than both, for they have "not seen the evil which is done under the sun" (4:2-3). What this astonishingly provocative statement as good as says is that the only good secular humanist is not even a dead one, but one who has never existed! Qoheleth is saying that from God's point of view that is as much hope and as much meaning as an under-the-sun life can provide. The tears of the oppressed cry out for something better!

What Can Little Hands Do? (4:4-6)

As if to suggest that a fair proportion of human achievement is gained at the expense of the oppressed, Qoheleth turns to the thought that envy is the engine of much of what the world regards as success. This in turn leads him to ask what attitude we have to work and achievement. With vivid simplicity, the alternatives are sketched in terms of three sets of hands and how they are used—or not used, as the case may be—in the pursuit of a happy and productive life.

Two Hands (4:6b)

"Two handfuls with toil" (4:6b) symbolize the grasping obsession with ever-growing affluence. The corporate raider restlessly scans the stock market for new acquisitions for his business empire; the workaholic slaves compulsively for his first million . . . and his second, too; and the yuppies maneuver themselves with calculated deftness toward the apex of the corporate ladders of our time. The common factor is an impenetrable preoccupation with personal advancement. What we *want*, we define in terms of *need*, and since it is inevitable that what we believe we need must be good, our personal goals, thus qualified, become the driving imperatives of life. Ambition becomes necessity; necessity becomes a god. In his penetrating study of the modern concept of need, Tony Walter shows how the abandonment of moral and spiritual obligation to God has led to the widespread assumption that "the individual himself or herself, and his closest loved ones, are seen as a person's ultimate frame of reference." Consequently, "meeting the needs of the self is increasingly talked of as life's project."[4] "Need is the religion of the religionless, the morality of those who pride themselves on having progressed beyond morality."[5] This is just the contemporary face of Qoheleth's "two handfuls with toil." Both hands are into possessions. That person is totally committed to the world's standard for success, and he is driven by "envy of his neighbor" (4:4).

Folded Hands (4:5)

Folded hands symbolize the position of the dropout. "The fool folds his hands and ruins himself" (4:5; Prov. 6:10). This is the opposite extreme from the rat race. He ruins himself—literally, eats his own flesh (which is what you do if you don't eat). His is a cannibalism of the whole man, body and soul. This at least has the advantage of being a quiet life—of a kind—but it is essentially self-destructive. And God's Word is clear that a man who "will not work . . . shall not eat" (II Thess. 3:10), while he who refuses to provide for his own family "has denied the faith and is worse than an unbeliever" (I Tim. 5:8). Strong words these, but no less dire than the consequences of indolence in the lives of the dropouts and their dependents. Escapism may feel good at the time, but it is no solution. The escapist has jumped from the frying pan into the fire.

One Hand (4:6)

There is another way. "Better *one handful with tranquility*" (4:6a). This beautiful expression is presented as a middle way between two-fisted grasping and hand-folding laziness. But it is far more than a balance between two extremes—it is a radical alternative to two essentially sinful positions. The idea is of a modest and contented life, in which one hand is put forth effectively and successfully but garners tranquility in the process. It is possible to have genuine peace *and* the prosperity with which God would reward our labors. But what is the other hand doing? The Bible says that the basic fact of the life of the Lord's disciples is that they are always with their Lord, who holds them by the "right hand" (Ps. 73:23). The condition of a happy balance in life is that the right hand—signifying our primary motive—be in the hand of our Father-God, while the left hand is put forth in fruitful and satisfying labor in commitment to the revealed purposes of God. A children's hymn by Henry E. Button is near to the mark, in spite of its overtones of middle-class sentimentalism.

> O what can little hands do
> To please the King of Heaven?
> The little hands some work may try,
> To help the poor in misery:
> Such grace to mine be given.

Every other approach is "chasing after the wind" (4:6c)!

Success Without a Successor (4:7-12)

Successful people are often lonely in the crowd. Ebeneezer Scrooge, in Charles Dickens's *A Christmas Carol*, was a sad and lonely man until Tiny Tim melted his miserly soul. Billionaire Howard Hughes ended his days a chronic recluse, haunted by his fears of disease—a living-death testimony to the impotence (or was it the danger?) of material prosperity in the face of profound spiritual darkness. Isolation is often the concomitant of worldly success. The amiable chatter at celebrity cocktail parties may only mask aching oceans of loneliness. Indeed, being in the presence of so much superficial conviviality only serves to underline the emptiness of such relationships, at least for those who long for genuine companionship.

Qoheleth brings these twin themes together—success and loneliness—in reference to a man who had no family to whom he could give support in his lifetime and leave his money after his death. He was torn between his overwhelming lust for greater wealth and the obvious senselessness of doing all this when he had no issue (4:7-8). He had good reason to ask the question, "For whom am I toiling?" (v:8). Avarice is always a hard, and less than rational, taskmaster! This man was a slave to moneymaking: it was a case of "the less need, the more raking."[6] And to the extent he was enslaved, he was, as Derek Kidner trenchantly observes, "virtually dehumanized, for he [had] surrendered to a mere craving and to the endless process of feeding it."[7] This is more obviously meaningless in view of his lack of dependents or heirs, but many children have had a father like him, and many a wife such a husband. They never saw him from one day's end to another, and when their paths did cross, it was as ships passing in the night. Qoheleth's workaholic at least had no family to neglect! His latter-day descendants will be buried in their work on the day when Christ returns to judge the living and the dead. This is what the worship of self can do to us!

It is as well to remember that Qoheleth was speaking to the people of God. Yes! It is very possible for Christians to throw themselves into disfunctional patterns of life. Devoted pastors have sacrificed their families on the altar of an exaggerated and unbalanced view of their calling. Christian businessmen can enjoy making money and find it a deal easier than the work of forging a healthy home life in loving and patient cooperation with wife and children. Some men live like bachelors all their married lives, to the eternal frustration of their wives and families. Not being alone means far more than merely having people that you can call loved ones or friends. The antidote to loneliness is practical companionship and the principle, as stated by Qoheleth, is that "two are better than one, because they have a good return for their work" (4:9). In a real partnership, the whole is better than the sum of its parts: if two is better than one, it is also better than both of the ones, when they are alone!

Four illustrations flesh out this idea and show us something of the practical blessings of companionship.

Friendship (4:9-10)

A friend in need—your need, not his—is a friend indeed. "If one falls down his friend can help him up. But pity the man who falls and has no one to help him up" (4:10). If you have had either experience, you know the force of Qoheleth's point. I learned something of this one bitter January in a rowing boat on the River Ythan in Aberdeenshire, Scotland. I was taking core samples of estuarine mud in connection with my research into the distribution of a species of annelid worm. As I sifted through one sample, the intense cold froze my hands and I fainted away, apparently in shock. When I came to, my friend Dick (who was looking for eider duck regurgitations in the same mud flat) was straightening me out in the bottom of the boat. I recall two things from that point until we got to the shore. One was his typically English understatement, when, with a chuckle he said, "Just as well you didn't fall *out* of the boat, old boy—I'd've had to row away without you!" The other was how thankful to God I was for such a friend, for that was the one thing he would never have done.

Warmth (4:11)

"If two lie down together, they will keep warm" (4:11). This is often taken to refer to a husband and wife, but it has, in fact, a wider reference. In days gone by, travelers used to bundle up close together at night for warmth. In the guard house at Old Fort Niagara, New York, you can see a bed on which 12 soldiers could sleep in their uniforms to keep warm and be ready for action if awakened by the sentries.

Security (4:12a)

Companions provide collective security. "Though one may be overpowered, two can defend themselves" (4:12a). The man who fell among thieves on the road to Jericho was alone. Today's bandits stalk the downtown streets of after-dark America.

Strength (4:12b)

The ties that bind give strength. "A cord of three strands is not quickly broken" (4:12b). The above illustrations focused on the advantages of two over one. Here a standard cord of three strands suggests that three will be better than two. In New Testament terms we are reminded of the two on the road to Emmaus who were joined by a third—the risen Christ—and could later testify how their hearts had burned within them as the Lord fellowshiped with them along the road (Luke 24:32). Jesus sent his disciples out in twos (Matt. 10:16), but it is always his presence as the invisible third companion that is the power lending wings to their witness (Matt. 28:18-20). The close intertwining of the three cords also suggests that it is not numbers as such, but the quality of the binding ties of fellowship that are of critical significance. Quality as opposed to quantity and personal commitment rather than mere strength in numbers are what make this companionship a profound blessing for those who enjoy it. Believers are "heirs *together* of the grace of life" (I Pet. 3:7). It is *in Christ* that *we* (together) shall be more than conquerors (Rom. 8:37). The sharing of our lives with one another flows from the one salvation in Christ our Savior (Acts 2:42; II Cor. 8:5). This rebukes the religious loner, "who belongs to no Church, because no Church is perfect enough for him,"[8] and calls us to a practical membership one with another. As with all Qoheleth's solutions to human problems, the answer leads ultimately to a life of faith in the Lord. Without that, life is truly an empty existence.

Life at the Top (4:13-16)

If money cannot insulate someone against loneliness, how about power and position? The answer is so obvious that it would seem more intelligent to ask why anybody would want to be a king or a president. Rulers soon find that the higher up a mountain you climb, the colder it gets. And how much less room there is at the top. The corridors of power are lonely places. Today's hero is tomorrow's pariah. The comforts of a good showing in the polls is fleeting at best.

Qoheleth tells the story of "an old but foolish king" who was supplanted by "a poor but wise youth," only to find that he too eventually fell into disfavor with his former supporters. He suffers what Herbert Leupold calls "the common fate of rulers."[9] Even in the relative tranquility of the Western democracies, where elections rather than military coups change the governments, political longevity is at the mercy of an electorate with an attention span of a few years at most. And landslide election victories are aptly named —real landslides are caused by shifting, unstable earth! This points to the vanity of thinking that political power or public acclaim will in itself somehow rise above the transience and meaninglessness of life lived under the sun. The few who are put into the position where, in theory, they should be able to implement their If-I-were-king ambitions find that they have reached "a pinnacle of human glory, only to be stranded there."[10] Mr. Pickwick might well sing (in the musical version of *The Pickwick Papers*), "If I ruled the world, every day would be the first day of spring," but the real world is something else and, anyway, the civil service wouldn't like it.

What is Qoheleth saying? That meaninglessness is inevitable in a life lived in terms of under-the-sun secularism. Oppression continues year after year, even human achievement owes more to envy than to altruism, and, in any case, wealth and power per se seem to exacerbate rather than ameliorate the emptiness that so many people feel. Although not stated by Qoheleth, the answer is to be found only in the living God. No one can read Ecclesiastes 4 without being driven back to chapter 3—to the conclusion that "every man may eat and drink, and find satisfaction in all his toil— this is the gift of God" (3:13). But to receive the gift, we must receive the Giver. And that's the rub for secular under-the-sun men and women!

Questions for Discussion

1. What is God's attitude to oppression (4:1)? What did Jesus experience (John 15:25), and what ought to be the Christian's response (Heb. 13:3; Luke 10:25-37)?

2. In what sense are the dead happier than the living (4:2-3)?

3. Why is "one handful with tranquility" (4:6a) to be preferred to two full hands (4:6b) and folded hands (4:5; see Prov. 6:10; II Thess. 3:10; I Tim. 5:8)?

4. What four examples prove that two (or three) are better than

one (4:9-12)? What insights can you glean from Luke 24:32; Matthew 10:16 and 28:18-20; and I Peter 3:7?

5. What is the lesson of the foolish king and the wise youth? Look back to 3:13.

5
HOLLOW RELIGION
Please Read Ecclesiastes 5:1-7

*Guard your steps when you go to the
house of God. Go near to listen rather
than to offer the sacrifice of fools, who
do not know that they do wrong.*

*Do not be quick with your mouth,
    do not be hasty in your heart
    to utter anything before God.
God is in heaven
    and you are on earth,
    so let your words be few.*

Ecclesiastes 5:1-2

In the popular mind, "religion" is an ugly word. "Religion" is, by and large, what other people "get," and "religious" is what other people are. Agnostics and evangelicals, if they agree on nothing else, will unite in denying that they have a religion. At the same time, the former will claim to have no faith while the latter will cheerfully confess a supernaturalist biblical faith in Jesus Christ. For the skeptics, all faith is religion and to be rejected as a mystical hoax. For Christian believers, faith is belief of the truth and a good thing, while religion is equated with nominal and outward formalism and is therefore a bad thing. This distinction goes back a long way. For example, the eighteenth century poet, Robert Burns, uses it to contrast the simple fervent faith of a Scottish cottager with the showy religiosity of the Establishment. Having described family worship as it was and still is practiced among godly Presbyterian folk in Scotland—the singing of a psalm, reading of Scripture, and kneeling for extempore prayer—he writes:

Compar'd with this, how poor Religion's pride,
   In all the pomp of method, and of art;
When men display to congregations wide
Devotion's ev'ry grace, except the heart!
The Power, incens'd, the pageant will desert,
The pompous strain, the sacerdotal stole:
   But haply, in some cottage far apart,
May hear, well pleas'd, the language of the soul,
And in His Book of Life the inmates poor enroll.[1]

Allowing for the fact that Burns was a Scot of Presbyterian lineage (and therefore had an intestinal aversion to anything that smacked of ritual and show) and was an Enlightenment man (who was a skeptic in matters of religion) it must still be admitted that he has a very valid point. There is a self-evident hollowness in much of what passes for Christianity in this world of ours. And as it was a stumbling block for Robert Burns two centuries ago, so it is today for millions of people within and without the borders of institutional Christianity.

How is God to be approached? How are we to worship and serve him? Where does God fit in the human experience? And what use is all the religion in this world, when it seems as if it's all going to hell on a rollercoaster? If God is supposed to be the solution to our deepest problems, why is there so much religion and precious little real faith?

Qoheleth has been concerned to show the meaninglessness of life lived under the sun—that is, without reference to God as the ultimate reality. In the course of this discussion he hints at the answer to the problem. There is the potential for joy and satisfaction, and it is in pleasing God (2:24-26). There is also the fact that God rules all of history and will judge in perfect righteousness (3:1-22). Yes, says Qoheleth, there is meaning in life, but it is only going to be found in a faith relationship to the Lord. Only in him can we understand correctly this world in which he has placed us. And only in him, can we cope with the challenges it presents. When we relate this to the emptiness of human lives and, specifically, the soul-destroying loneliness that so many people feel (4:1-16), we must see that the answer is to know the Lord personally as the friend "who sticks closer than a brother" (Prov. 18:24). He is the missing companion. He is the giver of life and of ultimate meaningfulness.

But Qoheleth is aware of the fact that religion and man's approach to God can be corrupted along with everything else in a sin-sick world. So how do his gentle pointers to an answer that says "Meaning will be found in true faith in God" mesh with the abounding evidence that so much religion seems little better than a charade and looks pretty meaningless itself? Is religion not also "a chasing after wind"? Qoheleth knows how easy it is for us to go through the motions, whether it is telling beads or singing hymns. He wants us to distinguish an empty, meaningless religion from the real thing. He wants us to root out formalism and come to experience living communion with the Lord. Consequently, he begins with that most fundamental element of Christian experience—the worshipers' approach to God. We could argue forever about theological positions and which denominations have the most biblical practice of worship. We could discuss, as Herbert Schlossberg has so brilliantly done, the ways in which the church has set aside God's Word in favor of embracing, promoting, and even idolizing the spirit of the age and the cultural norms or secular (i.e., under-the-sun) society.[2] But Qoheleth begins with your first step toward God. And he knows that no one can hide from such a question. After all, we all have a real, definable experience (or nonexperience) of worshiping God. We know, one by one, who we think God is, and we know well the attitudes we bring to our approach to him. Of course, Qoheleth is speaking primarily to the professed people of God. His point of contact is their actual piety, such as it might be. And his discussion penetrates behind the screen, as it so often is, of creedal definitions and theological shoptalk to lay the claims of God upon the conscience and demand a practical response, whether of faith or (God forbid!) unbelief. If your life seems to be meaningless, then realize that it is because meaninglessness in one form or another has a lodgment in your heart. Meaninglessness cannot be imposed from outside upon a heart that has been reborn by the Holy Spirit and reformed by saving faith in Christ. But, like any other manifestation of rebellion against God, it can be entertained and indulged as the Christian wavers in his faithfulness to Jesus Christ.

Approaching God (5:1-3)

Central to the Christian life is the principle that our *inward* obedience is to run parallel to our *outward* obedience.[3] When the latter is slowly eroding, as it was in Qoheleth's Israel (Neh. 13:10-20;
Mal. 1:8), it is clear that hearts are no longer turned to the Lord as
they ought to be. The Bible consistently addresses the necessity of
a careful outward conformity to God's will, built upon an inward
love and devotion toward him as a personal Father-God, in Jesus
Christ. From the heart to the hand, we are called to joyous discipleship. We are not to be like those who honor God with their
lips, while their hearts are far from him (Mark 7:6). Qoheleth,
then, has a message for the person who, as Kidner so neatly puts it,
"likes a good sing and turns up cheerfully enough to church: but
who listens with half an ear and never quite gets round to what he
has volunteered to do for God."[4]

Reverence (5:10)

We must never forget who God is. "Guard your steps when you
go to the house of God" (5:1a). The text says literally, "Watch your
feet." The same expression occurs in Isaiah 58:13, where we are to
keep our feet from breaking the Sabbath. The idea is that when we
are not careful to do God's will, we inevitably trample upon it.
Where we put our feet tells something about our attitude. We vote
with our feet! A related piece of symbolism is found in Moses' en-
counter with God at the burning bush. God instructed Moses to
remove his sandals, because the ground on which he stood was holy
(Exod. 3:5). Moses' feet must be clean in the presence of God—it
was an outward sign of an inward reverence for the living God.[5]

The "house of God" refers to the worship of God, preeminently
the temple in Jerusalem but perhaps also the local synagogues
throughout postexilic Judea.[6] Throughout the history of Israel, the
temple was where God revealed himself to his people in a palpable
manifestation of his glory. "Holiness adorns your house," said the
psalmist. "In reverence will I bow down toward your holy temple"
(Pss. 93:5; 5:7b). I believe that the recapture of a reverent approach
to the worship of God is an urgent necessity in the modern
church. It is not so much the structure of worship that need refor-

mation, as the attitudes we bring and the way we carry ourselves as we ostensibly come into God's presence. The preparation of the heart in quietness before the call to worship; the holy abandonment to full-throated praise; the bated breath of expectancy in prayer, punctuated by the "amens" of the soul, audible and/or inaudible; the sense of the Holy Spirit enveloping us in the act of worship, leading our hearts and minds to spiritual blessings in heavenly places in Christ (Eph. 1:3; 2:6); the joyous reception of the bread of life as the Word is opened; and the exultant celebration of our risen Savior as the blessing of God in Christ is poured out according to promise. For this to be a reality, we must be willing to concentrate our minds on the things above, not on earthly things (Col. 3:2). And only a clear view of the majesty of the God we worship will draw out such gripping, exhilarating reverence. God is our Creator, our Redeemer, and our Comforter. Every moment of living worship acknowledges this truth with joy.

A Ready Ear (5:1b)

We must listen to what God says. Ears come before lips in the order of Christian growth. "Consider carefully how you listen," said Jesus. "Whoever has will be given more; whoever does not have, even what he thinks he has will be taken from him" (Luke 8:18). Having presupposes listening and assimilating. Yet some Christians are so full of what they are going to share with others that there is little opportunity, or even inclination, to be quiet and hear what God is saying. "Be still, and know that I am God" (Ps. 46:10) must call forth the response, "I will listen to what God the Lord will say; he promises peace to his people, his saints—but let them not return to folly" (Ps. 85:8). The caveat is appropriate, for the problem of the Israelites was that too often "the message they heard was of no value to them, because those who heard did not combine it with faith" (Heb. 4:2). To go into God's presence and not hear what he is saying, is, says Qoheleth, "to offer the sacrifice of fools, who do not know that they do wrong" (5:1). It is irrational, if not indeed dangerous, to attend an audience with a powerful ruler and then willfully disregard all that he says. It is God who says that the sacrifice of the wicked is an abomination (Prov. 15:8).

His words are spirit and they are life (John 6:63). How we should hang upon his every utterance and take it to heart with thanksgiving!

Careful Words (5:2-3)

Likewise, we must guard our lips. "God is in heaven and you are on earth, so let your words be few" (5:2). Prayer is not to be blighted by hastiness or wordiness. Again the warning is against an empty formalistic type of praying. The Lord is not impressed by "babbling like pagans" or multiplication of prayers (Matt. 6:7; Isa. 1:15). "When words are many, sin is not absent" (Prov. 10:19). Unless we come to the Lord humbly, reverently and repentantly, "prayer is lost breath."[7] On the other hand, "the prayer of a righteous man is powerful and effective" (James 5:16). The spirit of true prayer was summed up by our Lord when he said to his disciples after the Last Supper, "If you remain in me and *my words remain in* you, ask whatever you wish, and it will be given you" (John 15:7, my emphasis). In the face of the severest threat to the fledgling church, the apostles and the believers held a prayer meeting (Acts 4:24-31). The record of that prayer is a marvelous practical example of what Qoheleth is enjoining upon us. The prayer is short. It begins with the worship and adoration of God (v. 24) continues with the application of Scripture to the precise problem facing the believers (vv. 25-28) and makes just one request (vv. 29-30). The answer followed with dramatic and powerful immediacy (v. 31).

Evangelicals are inclined to equate formalism in worship with time-honored rubrics, from the high liturgics of Rome to the "four walls and a sermon" of Presbyterians. Clerical garb, pipe organs, recited prayers, and programmed responses are seen as the cold tentacles of a cold and mechanical performance that simulates rather than expresses a lively approach to the worship of God. While there is, no doubt, some truth in this charge, it is not without the taint of a self-serving spirit. We may have escaped the ritual of the read prayers of the Prayer Book or the Pastor's Annual, but instead we find ourselves buried in a veritable landslide of prayer requests, many of them trivial and some of them verging on gossip. We don't recite prayers perhaps, but our "spontaneous" extempore prayers can be as ritually predictable (and not nearly as beautiful or profound) as, for instance, those of the old Anglican Prayer Book. This is not as much an argument for the latter as it is a caution against dead "spontaneity." In the same vein, guitar accompaniment becomes received orthodoxy and repetitive mantralike choruses are held as indicating a truly lively faith. Isn't it funny how it is always the other people who are needing to be liberated from forms and traditions? Truth is, it is too easy to trade new ritual for old and create a different formalism, the nature of which is masked by its initial novelty and seeming radicalism. My point is not to discuss the relative merits of these methods, but to emphasize that it is from the *heart* that issues of life proceed. There are certainly rights and wrongs, proprieties and improprieties, reverences and irreverences in the way we do our worshiping of God. But back of all these is the attitude of heart that gives them birth and expression. And crucial is a deep sense of who God is and our consequent felt need of his loving, merciful, gracious, and joyous fellowship in Jesus Christ.

Promises to Keep (5:4-6)

Whoever first expressed the mischievous idea that "laws are meant to be broken," might well have extended it to promises. It would perhaps be interesting, in a depressing kind of way, to know how many promises are made a day in these United States that are destined never to be kept. To come closer to home, we might narrow it to the undertakings that Christians make in context of the local church. How lightly, it seems, people say they will do something and then, when they either do it much later than they promised and only because of a reminder from someone else, or they never do it at all, resort to all sorts of special pleading in an apparent effort to justify their carelessness.

Of even deeper significance are the promises that people make to God and later do not keep. In the fellowship within which I minister, members are received on a profession of faith in Jesus Christ and make a "covenant of church membership" in which they solemnly promise to be a living part of the congregation of the Lord's people. We all promise to heed, in the Lord, the teaching and the discipline of the fellowship. We commit ourselves to Bible reading, prayer, keeping the Lord's Day, attending public worship, observing the sacraments, giving to the Lord's work, and ministering to one another and, most searchingly, to "forsake all sin" and conform our lives to the teaching and example of the Lord.[8] These are very normal and standard components of membership in the churches of the Protestant Reformation—so much so, that sometimes the "I dos" and "I wills" can roll off our tongues with relative ease. They are, nevertheless, profound commitments that are taken very seriously by the Lord and ought to so be taken by us.

When Qoheleth spoke of vows, however, he was not thinking so much of the promises, like membership vows, we make to keep what God commands of us anyway. To promise to do what he has specifically told us to do is only our reasonable service to him. Qoheleth had in mind voluntary vows that Old Testament believers made to God, especially in connection with the worship and sacrificial offerings of the temple. These could take any number of forms, from Hannah's dedication of a son to Jonah's reaffirmation of an earlier commitment to the Lord (I Sam. 1:11; Jonah 2:9). These were spontaneous and voluntary. God always required obedience but he did not require these specific vows. Scripture makes two clear rules about such vows: the first is that vows not be make hastily (Prov. 20:25); and the second is that when they are made, they are to be kept (Deut. 23:22-23). This is exactly Qoheleth's point.

Promises are to be kept. Not to keep a vow to God is to be a fool (5:4). Why a fool? Because God takes us at face value and will hold us to our solemn commitments. He will not tolerate pious language that is no better than a smoke screen for a deceitful heart and a treacherous hand. It is a fool who trifles with divine righteousness and thinks that God will wink at hypocrisy as if it is no more than a childhood prank!

Hence it is better not to make a vow at all, than to make one and not keep it (5:5). It is too easy to make big promises in the flush of some emotional experience; "do not let your mouth lead you into sin" (5:6a)! But it is not good enough to wiggle out of a solemn vow, as if it were no more significant than changing the times of an appointment with the dentist (5:6b). Why should we so lightly incur the just anger of God (5:6c)?

What is crucial here is, once again, the character of God and our personal relationship to him. At first glance, it may seem harsh for God to hold people to their vows. We are so used to broken promises that we tend to shrug them off with a bit of grumbling. We are often surprised when we find someone who is consistently conscientious and trustworthy. A society that takes for granted the easy making and breaking of promises naturally finds God's standards of uprightness rather hard to take. And that is just the point Qoheleth wants to get across: God is holy and cannot look upon sin, and those who are truly his believing people *want to do his will* from the depths of their renewed hearts! Believers hate sin and love righteousness. Their relationship with God does not consist in a set of external rituals and forms of words, but in heart commitment that issues in practical holiness. Believers *love* God and rejoice to do his will. God is good. He is full of grace. He keeps mercy for thousands but will by no means clear the guilty. He calls us to say what we mean and mean what we say. We have promises to keep.

The Awesome God (5:7)

Samuel Nesdoly recalls worshiping in the famous Moscow Baptist Church some years ago: "Especially touching was the message by an eighty-four-year-old saint. He reminded us, that for the Christian, fear of God involved the fear born of love: fear lest we should grieve our loving Heavenly Father."[9] This is exactly the right side of Qoheleth's statement of the alternatives: "Much dreaming and many words are meaningless. Therefore stand in awe of God" (5:7).

God is awesome. Before him, all the empty words and false assurance of empty religion will melt away. Ananias and Sapphira discovered that when they promised God one thing and then did another. Their deaths under the direct judgment of God stand as a monument in the New Testament age (as was the transformation of Lot's wife into a pillar of salt in the Old Testament period) to the impossibility of lying to God and thereby attempting to squeeze into God's kingdom with an unchanged heart and one's sins intact (Acts 5:1-11; Gen. 19:26; cf. Luke 17:32). Formalistic religion is meaningless before the Lord.

God is, however, awesome in his love. And he draws forth a loving response from all who, having received the Lord Jesus Christ as their Savior, know him as their Father-God who loved them and chose them "from before the creation of the world to be holy and blameless in his sight" (Eph. 1:4). And his love will not let us go. Living worship is simply the life of God in our hearts pouring forth: here in adoration and praise, there in confession of sin and tears of repentance; now in prayer for a deep concern, again in songs of thanksgiving for new life in Christ! Therefore stand in awe of God!

Questions for Discussion

1. Why must we guard our steps when we worship God (5:1; see also Exod. 3:3; Isa. 58:13)? Why do ears come before the tongue in the order of Christian growth (see Luke 8:18; Pss. 46:10; 85:8)?

2. Why should our words be few in our prayers (5:2-3; see also Isa. 1:15; Prov. 10:19; Matt. 6:7)? Discuss Acts 4:24-31 as a model of godly praying.

3. What are the two basic rules for voluntary vows (5:4; see also Prov. 20:25; Deut. 23:22-23)? Why is it better not to vow at all, than to make a vow and not keep it (5:5-6)?

4. How are we to relate to God (5:7; see also Luke 17:32; Acts 5:1-11; John 3:16; Eph. 1:14)? How is he to be worshiped (John 4:24)?

6

THE LOVE OF MONEY

Please Read Ecclesiastes 5:8-6:12

Whoever loves money never has money enough;
whoever loves wealth is never satisfied with his income.
This too is meaningless.

Ecclesiastes 5:10

There is an old English music hall song that sums up the unchanging inequities of this fallen world with that cheerful resentment so characteristic of the British working class.

It's the same the whole world over;
  it's the poor wot gets the blame.
It's the rich wot gets the plunder;
  Ain't it all a bloomin' shame?

Behind this ditty is a down-to-earth philosophy of life. It's a shame the way things are (but don't look for anything to change); the poor carry the country on their virtuous, hard-working, exploited shoulders (but virtue doesn't pay the rent, so who wants to be poor?); the rich are that minority of bloodsucking parasites on society (who get the plunder [a] that really belongs to the rest of us, [b] a share of which we are entitled to, and [c] that would obviously make our lives more enjoyable, or, to be highfalutin about it, more "meaningful").

There is more than a grain of truth in all this: there is, indeed, no virtue in being poor, and the oppression of the poor is a shameful, evil thing. The Bible says a lot about poverty and the poor. It nowhere romanticizes poverty into a kind of means of grace, as if poverty in itself commended sinners to God and eased their way into heaven by conferring some sort of merit upon them. What the Bible does speak about is that the poor and oppressed will find God to be their helper, when they turn to him in faith and seek his help in their troubles. And God will certainly judge all human sin and punish those who exploit and oppress their fellow human beings. And God calls his people to minister, practically and self-sacrificially, to those who are in need.

But in certain essential respects, it expresses something of the under-the-sun secular meaninglessness Qoheleth was striving to unmask, namely, the notion that wealth in itself is meaningful—a real answer to life's problems. Looking at it another way, there is an assumption abroad in the world that satisfaction may be found in wealth and that aspiring after greater riches is a good, normal, healthy activity. Certainly, no one would ever deny that an increase in personal income will relieve financial pressure (assuming it does not become an excuse for increasing expenditure and thereby maintaining or even increasing that financial pressure). Neither will anyone deny that material prosperity is a legitimate goal of work. Scripture sees such success as a blessing from God, although it also defines wealth as a stewardship under God, given so that it may be used to further God's work in the world. The general attitude to moneymaking in our society has little room for the biblical stewardship-blessing model of personal prosperity.

The thought of getting something for nothing is far more exciting. It is not a simple desire to escape subsistence that makes gambling— including state lotteries—a multibillion dollar industry in the most affluent country in the world. It is not a burning passion to be enabled to support missionaries at home and abroad that causes hearts to beat faster when the $10 million publisher's sweepstakes ad offer arrives in the mailbox! Instant wealth seems to promise instant happiness. It is a heady and intoxicating illusion, but its fruit partakes of the same substance as its root. "Easy come" becomes "easy go!"

And the idea of working for yourself, succeeding, and living what is so deceptively called "the good life," is equally exciting. It also has a genuine element of legitimate, even laudable, achievement to it, because God does call us to work and he does bless work with success. But human sin can turn gold to dross and make blessings into curses. Material prosperity, which starts out to be a blessing, can become a tyranny that casts a dark shadow over human lives. What is *good* can so easily become a *god*. And when that happens, *material* becomes an *-ism*.

From the problems of empty, purposeless lives and hollow, formalistic religion, Qoheleth naturally turns to the love of money and good things. If we need a reason for living (purpose) and if we have a need for spiritual assurance in the living of life (religion) — and these can be the subject of delusion and meaninglessness under the sun — then our desire to sustain and enjoy our daily life (money, wealth) is also bound to hold great potential for under-the-sun meaninglessness. Qoheleth is not opposed to wealth (as he makes clear in 5:18-20), but he warns against material*ism* in all its forms. It is as empty and meaningless as every other tenet of secular (under-the-sun) humanist faith.

Dissatisfaction Guaranteed (5:8-12)

In the parable of the sower, Jesus says that the seed sown among thorns "is the man who hears the word . . . and the *deceitfulness* of wealth chokes it, making it unfruitful" (Matt. 13:22). Why does our Lord say this? Surely it is because wealth promises more than it can deliver. Children, when approaching Christmas or a birthday, will vehemently insist that such-and-such toy is exactly what they need. They will assure us that it will really satisfy them. And we all know how ephemeral that satisfaction is. Two days after the opening of the presents, they are back to their old tried and tested playthings. We adults are perhaps more sophisticated in our tastes. We are practiced technicians in the quest for personal satisfaction. We are often able to articulate our most naked ambitions in the language of need and even altruism. This is where the "deceitfulness" attaches itself to the "wealth." The deceit is in the human heart, of course, and it consists in the notion that a particular level of wealth, or a specific acquisition, will confer a lasting satisfaction of heart and soul. But, as we all know, there is never a complete stamp collection, a perfect house, the best vacation ever, or a large enough multinational corporation. Today's goal becomes yesterday's base line. Unhallowed ambition never stops hustling. The carrot is always ahead of the donkey. Satisfaction is an *ignis fatuus*. And the fellow who is chasing it through increased wealth is, as W. G. T. Shedd once said, "trying to jump off his own shadow . . . the further he leaps, the further his shadow falls."[1] If we believe that throwing money at the problem of life will actually give it meaning, forget it! Remember what Jesus said about the deceitfulness of wealth! Dissatisfaction is guaranteed!

Qoheleth's development of this theme begins with a characteristically tenebrous observation on the perennial truth that "the rich get richer and the poor get poorer." He notes that where the poor are oppressed, the bureaucracy and the judiciary give it "the Nelson eye."[2] Then they and the king succeed in enriching themselves at the expense of the poor (5:8-9). It's all here: "justice and rights denied" (v. 8) and ascending tiers of officialdom at once fobbing off the pleading victim and passing on a share of the loot to shifty-eyed superiors. The punch line is "do not be surprised at such things" (v. 8). What else can you expect in a world where people live in disregard of the things of God? What else can secularism produce? It has no absolutes outside of itself. At best it has the shifting-sand relativism of the 51-percent vote and "public opinion" to render judgment on the currently acceptable moral standards. At worst, it is Idi Amin, Pol Pot, and the Emperor Bokassa I! Qoheleth hates injustice but he is totally realistic about the destructive potential of under-the-sun secularism. He "pins no hopes on utopian schemes or on revolution. He knows what is in man."[3] There is more than a suggestion here that the kind of motivation that drives people on to self-aggrandizement and a consuming passion for money inevitably multiplies misery and escalates excess. Is there a real prospect of materialism giving birth to lasting happiness in this world? Qoheleth says, in effect, "Don't hold your breath!" And that is only his introductory hint! He goes on to add three very explicit answers in the negative.

Never Enough (5:10)

"Whoever loves money never has money enough" (5:10). It's the getting, not the mere having, that is exciting. What we have is not enough. The fun, the kudos, the satisfaction, are in the act of acquiring what our heart desires. As in the days of the prophet Amos, we have to drink out of bigger and better cups and go to sleep on more expensive beds (Amos 6:4-6). That modern barometer of economic success, the standard of living, is not a fixed point, but a moving gravy train, which, for those who are on it, must keep on rolling.

Always a Bore (5:11)

Success is an anticlimax. When you finally acquire the things you want, they so often become a bore. You may own a Goya or a Gauguin, but you can only "feast [your] eyes on them" — enjoyable, no doubt, but hardly the quintessence of a meaningful life. Furthermore, "as goods increase, so do those who consume them" (5:11a). There are Hollywood stars who have scores of people in their retinue to help them cope with the demands of superstardom. Success always necessitates the recruitment of a staff to administer the growing establishment and its assets. This tends to take the gilt off the gingerbread. Expenses and overhead increase. Profit margins decline relative to gross income. Wealth has its own burdens.

No Real Security (5:12)

Wealth does not provide true security. Sir William Burrell (1861-1958) was a Scottish ship owner who devoted most of his long life to amassing a truly marvelous collection of art objects of all types and from all periods. A visit to The Burrell Collection, housed in a beautiful gallery in Pollok Park, Glasgow, is a most memorable excursion through world cultural history. Sir William gave his collection to his native city, but never lived to see it on permanent public view. He lived out his latter years as a virtual recluse in his home, Hutton Castle, in mortal fear of fire and theft consuming his life's work. The burden of his great work — which has preserved so much of our cultural heritage — was the torment of its manifest vulnerability. "The abundance of a rich man," says Qoheleth, "permits him no sleep!" (5:12b).

Jesus taught his disciples to put things—and he meant things that are good in themselves—in a divine perspective. Don't store up "treasures on earth," he said. After all, they are subject to decay and to theft. Rather, "store up for yourselves treasure in heaven, where moth and rust do not destroy, and where thieves do not break in and steal. For where your treasure is, there your heart will be also" (Matt. 6:19-21). Notice that this is not a proscription but a prescription. Earthly treasures had a place, but in perspective to their true value. In an under-the-sun outlook, an overestimation of material prosperity is unavoidable, because to a secular humanist, there is no heaven in which to store up the spiritual treasures that Jesus had in mind in the Sermon on the Mount. To be an earth-bound, under-the-sun humanist means that decay and theft nibble daily at the fragile meaning of your life. It is all you really have until and unless you receive the Savior who is Christ the Lord.

In Harm's Way (5:13-17)

On October 19, 1987, so-called "Black Monday," the New York stock market lost 23 percent of its paper value. A week or so later, Arthur Kane walked into an office in Miami, pulled a .357 magnum from his briefcase, killed the manager, maimed a broker, and committed suicide. The crash had all but wiped out a multi-million dollar portfolio, which he had built up with clever speculation but largely with borrowed funds. When Wall Street plunged, it imploded both the underpinnings of Kane's opulent lifestyle and, quite clearly, the very fabric of his being.[4]

Materialism is not merely a theory or a lifestyle, which, like a brand of coffee or a make of washing machine, is morally neutral and physically harmless. Materialism maims and kills. It has consequences that Qoheleth describes as "grievous" evils.

Is Hoarding Harmless? (5:13)

One man may hoard his wealth. This is "to the harm of its owner" (5:13b). But what harm? The text does not spell it out for us, but it gives us a clue—the notion of hoarding. If you ask your average miser why he hoards his wealth, he will tell you that he is not hoarding but saving. He is just being prudent in conserving his assets.

Well, is there a viable distinction between hoarding and saving? Or is it purely a matter of one man's meat being another man's poison? The biblical answer is defined by the purpose of wealth itself. Why does God give prosperity to people? Just so that we might, from our bounty, supply the needs of those who are truly indigent (II Cor. 8:13ff.) Money and goods are God's provision for our sustenance, but for the Christian who has such wealth they are also a channel of God's love that reaches out toward others. Biblical saving is never an end in itself, but a means toward a loving, outward-reaching end—that is, provision for real needs. Parents, for example, should save up for their children and not children for their parents (II Cor. 12:14).[5] Saving has definite God-honoring goals. The channeling, not the immobilization, of resources is in view. Saving takes its place in the spectrum of a dynamic scriptural spectrum of Christ-centered personal financial goals, which must include obedience in the areas of personal consumption, family support, giving to the Lord's church (tithing), debt (minimization and avoidance), and long-term provision (saving).[6] Saving is one component among many—and not a dominating one—in a life that is constrained and guided by a balance of biblical direction for the whole life. Hoarding, in contrast, is the heresy of which saving is the orthodoxy. The hoarder serves his hoard, the biblical saver serves his Lord!

The hoarder locks up resources that belong ultimately to God. He keeps them from God and, therefore, he keeps them from their true purpose. He is willing to starve men and women to keep his wealth intact. And, ironically, he even keeps them from himself! Misers *are* miserable!

What if You Lose It? (5:14)

What about the loss of wealth through some misfortune? This happens and it is a catastrophe for all involved, including the next generation. We expect progress, however modest at times; we find any drop in our standard of living a bitter pill at the best of times. Having to tighten our belts because of financial strictures is always a tremendous challenge. But what if the goal of our life is embodied in our wealth? What if all we hold dear is tied to our material prosperity? In that case, to lose it is to lose the central motive of life! You have nothing! Your children have nothing! You are lost and your life has come apart at the seams! Qoheleth is pleading for some candid stock-taking. Are you, as the devotional writers of past centuries put it, "lying light" to the things of this world? Are you willing to be poorer than you are, and still praise God for it? Are you willing to die to the messianic pretensions of wealth?

Does Wealth Bring Real Gain? (5:15-17)

Death is the great *terminus ad quem* of mammon's illusory comforts. "Naked a man comes from his mother's womb, and as he comes, so he departs. He takes nothing from his labor that he can carry in his hand" (5:15; cf. vv. 16, 17). He takes *something*—his heart, spirit, soul, conscience, and character; his relationship with God, whether for weal or woe—but he can take nothing in his *hand*. Shrouds don't have pockets! To live for wealth is simply futile. Where is the gain? He "eats in darkness" and there is "great frustration, affliction and anger!" (5:17). Qoheleth's assessment of the blandishments of materialism is, as Charles Bridges remarks, "a frowning cloud."[7] It is no less accurate and judicious for that melancholy fact.

Weighing the Alternatives (5:18-6:6)

Qoheleth's reverse psychology now takes us from that "frowning cloud" to a "bright vision," which is in fact his personal testimony.[8] His emphasis is vibrant with life. The Revised Standard Version accurately renders the Hebrew text: "Behold, what I have seen to be good and to be fitting is . . ." (5:18). He commands our attention. "Hear this," he says; "this is what you need to grasp!"

Life Is for Enjoying (5:18-20)

One of the great misconceptions that many people, including some very sincerely committed Christians, entertain about the Christian life is the notion that it is supposed to be rather somber and sorrowful. Not long ago, I attended a pastor's study conference. During the question time after one of the presentations, the speaker somehow took us from the necessity of reverence in worship to a blanket condemnation of smiling during a worship service! For him, the only proper attitude for the worship of God was an unbroken seriousness, if not indeed strickenness, of both spirit and visage! Regrettably, this pastor has not been alone in this opinion. Like dripstone forming in a limestone cave, this straitened joylessness has built up a cold calcified overlay on the lives of many Christians such that they feel inhibited about enjoying the good gifts of God and giving vent to it in praise to God.

Scripture teaches the exact opposite. The Lord turns mourning into dancing for those he saves from their sins. He calls us to rejoice in his gifts. We are promised that there is real satisfaction for us in our labor, however toilsome it may be. He rolls back the effects of the man's fall into sin—the curse of Genesis 3:17—and redeems the whole life of his people. He sent his only-begotten Son to die an atoning, substitutionary death for the sins of every sinner that he will save for himself. Rejoicing is the *only* appropriate response and ought to pervade every aspect of the Christian's devotion to the Lord. Sometimes there will be tears, but they will be out of joy as well as grief.

The key word in Qoheleth's argument is the name of God. God has given us our "few days" (5:18). God has given wealth and the ability to enjoy it (5:19a). God gives happiness in our work (5:19b). God sustains his people with "gladness of heart" (5:20). To receive the gift for what it is presupposes believing and trusting in the Giver. The godless enjoyment of the good gifts of God's world is an empty parody of the blessings experienced by the Lord's people as they glory in the goodness of their heavenly Father. "All things are yours," says Paul to the Christians in Corinth, "whether . . . the present or the future—all are yours, and you are of Christ, and Christ is of God" (I Cor. 3:21-22; cf. I Tim. 4:3-5). The Christian exults, "This is my Father's world. He has sent Jesus to be my Savior. He has given me eternal life and I shall never perish. And he provides for me every day with his goodness. Praise God, from whom all blessings flow! Praise Him, all creatures here below. Praise Him above you heavenly host! Praise Father, Son, and Holy Ghost!"

Count the Cost (6:1-6)

Think about what you lose when you go the world's way. God actually showers his gifts upon people of all sorts and conditions. There is a common goodness of God to the human race whom he created to be his image bearers in the world. Many people have their heart's desire (6:2a). The rich young ruler and the eponymous antiheroes of the parables of the rich fool and the rich man and Lazarus are clear examples of this in the New Testament (Luke 18:18-30; 12:13-34; 16:19-31). For many, there is something missing. They never quite get to enjoying it as they would like. Qoheleth attributes this to the hand of God (6:2b). Sometimes their wealth falls to a stranger (6:2c). Another has many children, but is so reviled by them that he is not even accorded a decent burial (6:3).

Surely, says Qoheleth, this is meaningless. Here you are, living out your life under the sun—no God, no future beyond the grave, no certainties in this life, excepting its uncertainties and its short-ness, and plenty of pain and frustration in the meantime. A still-born child is better off! It comes and goes and is forgotten; and in under-the-sun terms it has more peace than the fellow who slaves away for years—even supposing he lived 2,000 years—yet fails to enjoy his prosperity (6:4-6a)!

The argument is relentless and irrefutable. We all know that if this life is all there is, then it is undeniable that the billionaire and the stillborn baby "all go to the same place" (6:6b). Death ends whatever meaning there might have been. Is this the basis on which you want to live out your days? Is this all that you can make of the world around you? Is this your response to the manifest evidence of God's existence, goodness, and claims upon your life?

Postlude: Think on These Things (6:7-12)

Qoheleth has been reflecting on three significant problems relative to the meaning of life—a general feeling of purposelessness in life (4:1-16), the hollowness of formalistic religion (5:1-7), and the futility and frustration of a materialistic love of money and things (5:8-6:6). Obviously, this is neither a systematic nor a comprehensive treatment of the problems confronting human society. They are sufficient, however, to get people thinking, and that is Qoheleth's purpose. If we will but face a few facts in the light of God's gracious plan and purpose to redeem human lives from self-destruction and eternal loss, then will not every thought become captive to the Savior as the realization of truth is applied progressively to every aspect of life and thought?

In a postlude, therefore, Qoheleth wafts some of the leading thoughts of his three-chapter pericope on problems across the (one hopes) agitated waters of our minds. It is as if he is saying: "Think on these things! Don't let them escape. Don't shrink from the issues. Wrestle with them and, as Jacob wrestled with God at Peniel (Gen. 32:22ff.), refuse to let them go without a blessing and a happy resolution."

Review the implications of under-the-sun life. The purpose of our endless work still seems elusive. On the face of it, our physical appetite dictates what we do, and yet we never get to the point where it is satisfied. We have to keep on keeping on . . . apparently forever (6:7)! Does the wisdom of the Ph.D. and the bootlicking servility of the poor really make them any better off in the end (6:8)? No, says Qoheleth, "better what the eye sees"—that is, the enjoyment of the real gifts God has given to us—than the "roving of the appetite," the chasing of unhallowed and unsatisfiable desires (6:9).

The truth is that the human thirst for autonomy over against God is a phantasm (6:10-12). There is "one who is stronger than [we]," with whom "no man can contend" (6:10). Who can dispute with God? "Woe to him who quarrels with his Maker," thundered the prophet. "Does the clay say to the potter, 'What are you making?' " (Isa. 45:9). Our limitations are so obvious that any pretensions to godlike autonomy are almost laughable. The more we talk, the less meaningful are our words. "Who knows what is good . . . ?" (6:12). Under-the-sun man has no absolutes to guide him. Take away G-O-D and "good" becomes a big round O—there is no standard except the most recently triumphant philosophical and ethical fad. And how long will that last? As to the future, "who can tell him what will happen?" (6:12). There are no certainties either. No promises. No milestones along the way to the nonexistent goals of this under-the-sun world. Only fears about pollution, the ozone layer,

nuclear war, third world debt, and the economy. What can you
really live for if that is the way of things? What value is your wealth
in such a context? Qoheleth "is slamming every door except the
door of faith."[9] In the fullness of New Testament revelation, Paul
would tell the apostolic church that "the Scripture declares that
the whole world is a prisoner of sin, so that what was promised,
being given through faith in Jesus Christ, might be given to those
who believe" (Gal. 3:22). There is just no other way.

Questions for Discussion

1. What happens to so much of the fruit of honest toil (5:8-9)?
Why is wealth deceitful (Matt. 13:22)?

2. Can materialism give lasting happiness (5:10-12)? Discuss the
three answers in these verses and compare them with Jesus' answer
in Matthew 6:19-21.

3. Is materialism a "victimless" pursuit (5:13-14)? Compare hoarding with the Bible's view of using wealth (II Cor. 8:13ff.; 12:14).

4. What basic truths put wealth in balanced perspective (5:15-17)?

5. Identify two alternatives to materialism in 5:18-6:6 and discuss
what this implies for the way we are to live our lives. What does
the Preacher think about this (6:7-11)?

PART THREE
ANSWERS

7
LEARN FROM EXPERIENCE!
Please Read Ecclesiastes 7:1-14

Sorrow is better than laughter,
because a sad face is good for the heart.
The heart of the wise is in the house of mourning,
but the heart of fools is in the house of pleasure.

Ecclesiastes 7:3-4

*E*xperience is a great teacher, it is said. Alas, even the greatest of teachers have run up against some less-than-great learners! These are not necessarily in the minority either. There is little evidence that mankind is breaking out of his long-standing habit of repeating the mistakes of the past. It sometimes seems as if every generation has to reinvent the wheel in terms of public morals and personal ethics. The appreciation of the lessons of history—history is, after all, the only real mediator between past mistakes and present decision making—does not come very naturally to the young and the restless. When we are young we are looking to get experience for ourselves and we tend to be impatient with the advice of our elders. We too easily imagine that *we* will do things properly. We boldly comfort ourselves with the thought that, should we stumble and fall, this would only be par for the course—don't we all have to make our own mistakes anyway?

Wise and experienced elders may seethe a little at such attitudes. But youthful inexperience aside, there is a core of truth in this position, for it remains a fact of life that we learn many, if not most, of our best lessons through our personal and often painful experiences of setback and failure. It must also be admitted, however, that this is often a case of learning the hard way! And it surely goes without saying that ignoring the lessons that may be gleaned from the experiences of others is hardly a wise way to proceed in life.

Because the Bible is the inscripturated revelation of God's Word to mankind, it is the ultimate authority in matters of faith and life. It follows that were more people to heed it with spiritual discernment and intelligent devotion, there would be more learning through good experiences than bad! But God's Word always reckons with realities. Among these is the fact that we sin and do stupid things. Another reality is that troubles will come into our lives unbidden by anything we have said or done. God fills our lives with experiences through which he means to teach us and lead us to practical wisdom and spiritual maturity. The Holy Spirit was sent to the New Testament church to be our Helper, Comforter, and Counselor who would lead us into "all truth" (John 14:26). His work is never a mere intellectual transaction, like learning facts from a textbook, but is a practical course in which he brings the Word of God to bear upon our real experiences. The world *is* a school of hard knocks—and God uses it to bring us to Christian maturity.

This theme—learning from experience—is taken up in Ecclesiastes 7. Hitherto, Qoheleth's focus has been very much on the dark side of the world's problems—specifically purposelessness (4:1-23), formalistic religion (5:1-7), and materialism (5:8-6:12). Now he addresses himself to the answers we so desperately need. He begins with a series of proverbs, in which he successively speaks of the value of hard experiences (7:1-6), points to potential hindrances (7:7-10), and points to the need of a God-centered wisdom to cope with life (7:11-14).

Responding to the Hard Things of Life (7:1-6)

Nowhere in human experience is there a wider gap between theory and practice than in the way we respond to personal difficulties. It is so easy to trot out some cutesy piece of bravado like "When the going gets tough, the tough get going"—especially when somebody else has been hit by a serious problem—only to crumble into a crushed paralysis of spirit oneself, when waylaid by a personal setback. We all want everything to go smoothly and easily.

And such an aspiration is thoroughly biblical and is a very appropriate focus of our prayers for ourselves and others. "Make it your ambition," said the apostle Paul, "to lead a quiet life, to mind your own business . . . so that your daily life may win the respect of outsiders" (I Thess. 4:11-12). Nevertheless, there are certain givens about life in the real world—and one of them is that sooner or later we will run into something that is neither of our choosing nor to our liking. If we are to respond positively to these difficulties, if and when they arise, we will need to be prepared for them. At the very least, we will need to be persuaded that there is some possibility of redeeming such experiences so that defeats may be turned into victories.

Funerals Are Better Than Birthdays! (7:1-4)

The first of Qoheleth's two examples is, not surprisingly perhaps, that most inevitable of inconveniences in life . . . *the fact of death.* He begins with a most amazing statement: "A good name is better than fine perfume, and the day of death better than the day of birth" (7:1). Our immediate response is to ask what, if anything, these two sayings have to do with one another. They seem to be entirely unrelated ideas, at least to Westerners. To the Hebrew, however, there was a rich parallelism in the conjunction of these seemingly disparate thoughts. To have a good name is better than fine perfume because the former represents something of the inward essential nature of a person—reputation and integrity. Perfume, on the other hand, is just on the surface—an often delightful but essentially outward and cosmetic effect. To reverse the image, I am reminded of a Scotsman's comment on a hopelessly over-made-up woman: "If it takes that much manure," he cracked, "it cannae be verry great soil underneath!" A good name tells us something that a gallon of Chanel No. 5 never will. In a similar way, Qoheleth is suggesting, the "day of death" is better than "the day of birth." Why? Because the day of death—not just the future day when we each pass into eternity, but the repeated days of bereavement we go through when loved ones and dear friends die—focuses our minds on the crucial, ultimate questions of the meaning of life and the prospect of eternity. It isn't that remembering birthdays and having birthday parties are bad things—not at all. It is just that in the prospect of death our minds are concentrated — if we let them — on the most basic realities of our lives. Paradoxically perhaps, it is *death* that reaches into our deepest being and molds the very pattern of future life, while *birth* represents a backward-looking sentiment, devoid of power to channel what we will do with the years that are left to us.

This calls for explanation for the obvious reason that it is not self-evident that funerals are better than birthdays! Death is the very thing from which we naturally shrink! Qoheleth offers two explanations.

First, he argues that *death actually and practically helps us to think about life* (7:2). This is the principal value of funerals, and you will notice that it is also the antithesis of morbid introspection. It is the opposite of the satanic preoccupation with death so pervasive in the horror genre of movies and literature. Bereavement calls the thoughtless to think about realities in a way that parties and fun never will. Death knocks away the props and planks with which people shore up empty lives. Death reminds us of the realities that we succeed at other times in blotting out of our minds. And this is because "every funeral anticipates our own."[1] From this perspective, the tragically unwelcome intruder also carries an overture of grace from the outstretched hand of God. It is his grace that takes the devastating evil that death is in itself and lays it on our hearts in such a way as to make us think . . . perhaps bring us to pray out of a sense of our need . . . and even bring us to fellowship with Jesus Christ, who died to kill death for all who would simply believe in him as their Savior.

To be ready to die is to be ready for life and living! This is why Paul could say, "For to me, to live is Christ and to die is gain" (Phil. 1:21). What is his argument? It is just this: because he is ready to die, in Christ, and that would be eternal gain, so his whole life can be wonderfully lived out in discipleship to his risen Savior. This is the central glorious paradox of the Christian life. Make me a captive, Lord, and then I shall be free! The first shall be last and the last shall be first. He that is least in the kingdom of heaven shall be the greatest, and he that is greatest, the servant of all. In the midst of death we see life. His — Jesus' — strength is made perfect in our weakness. "Dying," said the apostle Paul, "we live." Qoheleth is in perfect harmony with the universal teaching of Scripture, when he says, "It is better to go to a house of mourning than to go to a house of feasting, for death is the destiny of every man; the living should take this to heart" (7:2).

Second, *sorrow deepens a person's innermost being* (7:3-4). Again we see the paradox—true happiness and joy are deepened and developed through the sorrows we may undergo. The point is not that we should be as sad as we possibly can be, as if, like endless doses of castor oil, this will do us a lot of good. There is no virtue in adopting a martyr complex. Sorrows are enemies, not friends. They are the rivulets that flow into the ocean of death. And like death, they must be conquered and turned around to some positive purpose, or they will consume us altogether. There is no need to beg trouble or to create difficulties for ourselves. Those that come along in the normal course of events are sufficient to test our faith. For the child of God, they can be a means of drawing us closer to the Lord. "Weeping may remain for a night, but rejoicing comes in the morning" (Ps. 30:5). Joy is the redemptive side of sorrow. Rita Nightingale learned this as she sat in the secluded shade underneath the hospital building in Lard Yao prison in Bangkok (the building was on stilts). Rita had been imprisoned after drugs were found in luggage she was carrying for a boyfriend. In the despair and discomfort of that Thai jail, she was led to faith in Christ. She had bitterly complained about the injustice of men and God in bringing her to such a sorry pass. But through the witness of women missionaries who visited her and especially that of Robert Laidlaw's famous tract, *The Reason Why*, given to her by an elderly lady from her hometown in England, she came to experience the freedom of the gospel of Christ. She realized that she had left God out of her life and that he, in his great love, had pursued her through the miseries of her imprisonment precisely so that she could be saved from her sins and brought to new life. "Eventually," she records, "I emerged from under the hospital hut and went inside it. I sat down in the waiting area and gazed out across the compound, blinking in the suddenly bright sunlight. *It's not just us who are in prison*, I suddenly thought. *The whole world's in prison, and I've just been shown the way out. I've been in prison all my life.*"[2] After reading a borrowed Bible that evening, she could say with simple sincerity of heart, "I closed the Bible feeling happy. I might not know much about God, but now I knew who he was."[3]

Rebuke Is Better Than Song (7:5-6)

A second major species of personal experience that can be felt most keenly is that of *admonition* or *rebuke*. "The wounds of the soul," writes James W. Alexander, "are not always such as bleed outwardly, nor is the most poignant anguish caused by visible agents." When someone rebukes us in any way, he says, "there is always an emotion of unhappiness."[4] Even when we know we are in the wrong and are sure that the person is rebuking us in genuine love, we feel the pain. We may be kicking ourselves, but we often feel like lashing out at others as well! It hurts at the best of times!

How are we to deal with such hurt? What does God have in it for us? Surely that we would change our ways. But also that we might value this correction as a privilege and a good gift. "It is better to heed a wise man's rebuke than to listen to the song of fools" (7:5), says Qoheleth. It is better, of course, because what he says is right and ought to be heeded for our own and everybody else's good. But it is better for at least two other reasons.

One is that *it takes love*, as well as wisdom, for a wise man to rebuke someone who is on the skids of error and who may even be careening toward self-destruction. Many a pastor has been praised for his excellent sermons, but none was more encouraged by a parishioner's comment than the preacher who was told by one of his congregation that the thing that had impressed him most forcibly from week to week was the fact that he—the pastor—loved his people so much as to tell them the truth! Such love ought to be returned with loving gratitude. A young man, a student for the gospel ministry, had to deliver a sermon before his presbytery.[5] After he had delivered it, the pastors and elders had opportunity to make comments on it and vote to sustain or not sustain. Generally the comments were positive, but one pastor, while commending the seminarian, remarked that for all that was good and scriptural in the sermon, it had in fact missed the central point of the Bible text that had ostensibly been explained. He explained this key concept in a few words and commended it as a point for future consideration. Many years later, the two men—the pastor and the seminarian, now a pastor—ran into one another at a church meeting and got to reminiscing about years past. "Do you remember that time when you criticized my sermon before the presbytery?" the second man said. "I was so angry at the time, it just burned me up to be told I'd missed the point. Well, some years later—in my pastorate—I decided to preach on that text. So I dusted off my student sermon and read it over. And as I reviewed it, all that you had said that day came back to me, and as it did, I realized that you had been absolutely correct and my anger had been totally unjustified! Thank you for making such a searching comment, and let me encourage you never to shrink back from telling people what they need to hear from God!" Be thankful for a wise counselor, for "better is open rebuke than hidden love. The kisses of an enemy may be profuse, but faithful are the wounds of a friend" (Prov. 27:5, 6).

Another, and compelling, reason to listen to the rebuke of a wise counselor, is that *the alternative is bad news*. Listening to "the song of fools" might well be appealing but could hardly be a sure-footed guide to unraveling the intricacies of life. The very expression "the song of fools" conjures up images of the happy hour when the drinks flow and the most threadbare of jokes can raise a roistering laugh. This is like "the crackling of thorns under the pot" (7:6). There is a Hebrew pun in this expression. The *sirim* (thorns) crackle under the *sir* (pot).[6] And the music of the language takes a tilt at the burning of an inferior fuel—thorns rather than the normal charcoal—that is more sound than substance, more show than solidarity. This represents the character of foolishness and flattery. It warns against the false promises of the easy way out. "Woe to you who laugh now," Jesus taught his followers, "for you will mourn and weep" (Luke 6:25). Some imagine that they can drown their sorrows and escape from the challenges of life in carousing and conviviality. But after the last hurrah, it's back, as the Scots say, to "old clothes and porridge." The world is still there. And it won't go away. That is why a rebuke from a wise and loving friend is worth the pain it necessarily inflicts. "No discipline is pleasant at the time, but painful. Later on, however, it produces a harvest of righteousness and peace for those who have been trained by it" (Heb. 12:11).

Overcoming Hindrances (7:7-10)

The trouble with the school of hard knocks is that the bruising can too easily crowd out the learning and retard personal growth. Trials can burn us out. Setbacks can crush a person's spirit. But to be forewarned is to be powerfully forearmed. Just knowing what is happening to us gives us an opportunity to respond—perhaps to take avoiding action, certainly to pray for God's help. Qoheleth alerts us to four possible hindrances to personal growth.

Pressure (7:7)

The first may perhaps be identified with what we today call pressure. The "extortion" that makes "a wise man into a fool" and the "bribe" that "corrupts the heart" (7:7) represent the power other people can exercise to manipulate and dominate us and to destroy our integrity and individuality. Oppression, not excluding temptations to sin, tends to dehumanize in the sense that it enslaves and corrupts its victims. Succumbing to pressure undermines the moral foundations of our convictions and value systems and steadily erodes that sense of balance and proportion with which we order our lives. People under pressure can feel driven to desperate and even suicidal actions. Qoheleth's warning is to identify and retreat from pressure as it encroaches on your life.

Impatience (7:8)

The second pitfall is an impatient attitude. Qoheleth emphasizes that "the end of a matter is better than its beginning" (7:8a). His point is that we look at the goal, not at the hurdles we are presently trying to negotiate. The trial of our faith, after all, is designed to produce patience (James 1:2-4) and to issue in greater, even eternal, triumph (II Cor. 4:17; I Pet. 5:9-10). "Patience is the child of faith."[7] Impatience is the bastard offspring of self-worship. Hence, Qoheleth's contrast: "patience is better than pride" (7:8b). Pride is essentially self-worship. Pride may well get us off to a confident start, but only patience will pull us through the rough spots.

Frustration (7:9)

The third danger is perhaps an extension of the foregoing point, a tendency to outrage when things do not go according to plan. We live in a day when outrage is regarded as a virtue. The ski masks worn by demonstrators and rioters of our cities have become the badges of modern righteous indignation. *Not* to raise your fist at the slightest provocation is to risk being regarded as a wimp. And in the media age, the presence of TV cameras virtually assures extravagantly aggressive behavior from demonstrators. Ours is the age of the short fuse—litigation at the drop of a hat, violence on the strike picket lines, histrionics in the check-out line, death in the streets; all are the symptoms of a society in which frustration has become the justification for instant vengefulness. That such anger is bound to be counterproductive and can only escalate the cycle of frustration and anger to greater and more lethal intensities is palpably obvious. It is, as the Scriptures repeatedly assert, bound up with foolishness in the human heart (7:9b; Prov. 14:17, 29; 15:18; 16:32). And James's corrective has urgent relevance: "Everyone should be quick to listen, slow to speak and slow to become angry" (James 1:19; cf. Eccles. 7:9a).

Vain Regrets (7:10)

A fourth and final hindrance to learning from our experience is vain regret that harks back to "the [good] old days" (7:10). Qoheleth is not saying that history is bunk. He is not suggesting that the study of history is a bad thing. Neither is he decrying the enjoyment of happy memories of days gone by. What he is concerned about is the kind of discontent that longs to turn back the clock to some alleged golden age in the past. My barber from college days appreciated this distinction. He was a homespun philosopher who reflected on life and history. One day he remarked that "in the old days, the ships were made of wood and the men were made of iron. But today? The ships are made of iron and the men are made of wood!" He was not suggesting a return to the good old days of Napoleonic naval engineering, but he was making an astute observation about modern man.

Pining for the glory days, as they imagined them, was one of Israel's recurrent failings—always in times of difficulty. During their wanderings in the Sinai desert, they even longed for their slavery in Egypt (Exod. 16:3; Num. 11:5-6; 14:1-4). Christians are not immune to this temptation. People enmeshed in the convoluted responsibilities of middle life look back to the carefree days of youth or college and the happy camaraderie of new and variegated friendships. There are people who never recover from the loss of what they believe were indeed the happiest days of their lives. There are other Christians who long for the excitement of their earliest experiences as new converts to Jesus Christ and feel the rest of their lives to have been anticlimactic. There are whole churches that steep themselves wistfully in their history, when they were more influential and seemed to be specially blessed with gospel power.

To think this way, says Qoheleth, is "not wise" (7:10b). Why unwise? Simply because past days, however palmy, are gone beyond recall. To learn from the past is good, as is the desire for the fullness of God's blessing now and in the future. But to pine after the past is to attempt to live life in reverse. Your real life is now and in the future. Your experience, past and present, must drive you forward to seek the Lord's blessing in the application of lessons learned, not backward to embittered dreams of vanished joy. God has, after all, given his believing children a personal faith in Christ which, as they receive the goal of their faith, fills them with "an inexpressible and glorious joy" (I Pet. 1:8). It is this irreducible joy in the heart of the Christian that can enable him to gain the victory over the bad times and the temptations to look back and come to the place of the apostle who could brush aside the severest troubles as "light and momentary" and declare them to be achieving for him "eternal glory that far outweighs them all" (II Cor. 4:17).

Wisdom from God (7:11-14)

God-given wisdom is the key to redeeming the multifaceted experiences of life. As we shall see in the next chapter, Qoheleth will show us how this wisdom can be acquired and developed. In the present context, he wants to emphasize that wisdom is "a good thing," which benefits those who see the sun" (7:11). How, in a nutshell, does this work out? Well, says Qoheleth, it is a shelter—like, for example, money. You all know how having money can shelter you in a most practical way from nasty things like hunger and cold. Wisdom is like that, only more so, for it "preserves the life of its possessor" (7:12). The point is that wisdom is a species of wealth that transcends the under-the-sun world and reaches to heaven. Or, rather, true wisdom reaches *from* heaven, from the Lord, and equips the believer with the resources to live a full and God-honoring life. To underscore this, Qoheleth reminds us that our lives are indeed lived under the hand of God (7:13-14). We are back to Ecclesiastes 3 and the biblical doctrine of the providence of God. The base-line presupposition of a faith that centers in the sovereign God is that our life—and the whole world—is in his hand. He knows the end from the beginning; he is absolutely sovereign; and he even marks the fall of a sparrow (Isa. 46:10; Dan. 4:34-35; Matt. 10:29). Our life also follows the arrow of time—from birth to the future. But it is not always a perfectly straight line. It is crooked at points. Sometimes these are little blips and at other times wide detours. The vital point is that the purpose of God is being worked out in both the straight and the crooked. So Qoheleth asks, "Who can straighten what he [God] has made crooked?" (7:13). God is dealing with us through the whole of our life's path. It follows that when times are good we should "be happy" and when problems arise we should "consider" (7:14). In that little gem of Christian spirituality, *The Crook in the Lot*, Thomas Boston outlines the method by which this considering will bear fruit in our hearts. Speaking of our response to a particularly hard experience, he encourages us to "consider it as the work of your God in Christ. This is the way to sprinkle it with Gospel grace. . . . The discerning of a Father's hand in the crook will take out much of the bitterness of it and sugar the pill to you. For this cause it will be necessary (1) Solemnly to take God for your God, under your crook, Psalm 142:4-5. (2) In all your encounters with it, resolutely to believe and claim your interest in Him, I Samuel 30:6." Then go on, says Boston, to consider who God is—as "your Father, elder Brother, Head, Husband, etc., who, therefore, surely consults your good." Consider also what it is that he is teaching you—perhaps correcting some sin, preventing some inadvisable course of action, deepening your self-awareness, and molding your character to be more like Christ.[8]

God is doing all things well. His timing is perfect. His goal is the highest possible good for all who love him. If there are bends in our road, they are the "rough ground" that "shall become level . . . for the mouth of the LORD has spoken" (Isa. 40:4-5).

Questions for Discussion

1. Why is the day of death better than the day of our birth (7:1-4)? Tie this in with what Paul says in Philippians 1:21 and II Corinthians 6:9.

2. When are hard words to be regarded as good things (7:5-6; Prov. 27:5-6)? What is the basic principle governing the Christian's hard experiences (Rom. 8:28; Heb. 12:11)?

3. What four pitfalls are we warned about in 7:7-10?

4. Why do we need wisdom, and where will we find it (7:11-14; see also Isa. 46:10; Dan. 4:34-35; Matt. 10:29)?

8

WISE UP!

Please Read Ecclesiastes 7:15-8:1

Who is like the wise man?
Who knows the explanation of things?
Wisdom brightens a man's face
and changes its hard appearance.

Ecclesiastes 8:1

The seminarian had a problem. His systematic theology paper was due by noon on Friday, and he hadn't the slightest hope of finishing it in time. So he decided, with a most lamentable dishonesty, to submit what he had done with some blank pages at the end to simulate the thickness of a completed paper. He would put it on the professor's desk and hope that he would leave the papers there over the weekend without looking at them, beyond noting who had turned them in on time. This had happened on other occasions, so he felt it to be a reasonable risk. First thing on Monday, he would come in early with the missing section and replace the blank pages. By noon that Friday, phase one of the deception was put into operation. The incomplete paper was on the prof's desk. He just hoped the plan would work. Less than an hour later, however, an angry professor tracked him down in the library, demanding not only an explanation for the blank pages, but also slapping a 5 P.M. final deadline for the rest of the paper! His deception in ruins and a serious question mark raised about his personal integrity as a Christian, the student got to work to redeem the extra time he had been given. After a while he just couldn't do any more. He had to take a break. So he slipped out of the building and ducked around the corner to a little coffee house. As he sat there nursing his coffee, his weariness, and maybe his shame, he looked up . . . and who should be coming into the coffee house, but the prof himself! Even before his mentor spotted him, he was on his feet and running out the door! But as he passed the astonished teacher, he plaintively (and with an irreverent disregard for its true meaning) muttered the words of the psalmist, "Whither shall I flee from thy presence!"[1] There was no escape. It was back to hitting the books. He completed both the paper and the course, but never became a pastor.

People may run away from problems, but problems never run away from people. Evasion didn't work for the seminarian in our story. Escapism doesn't make the world go away—it's still there after the hangover or the drug trip. Emigration doesn't work—the grass isn't greener on the other side of the hill. Even eremitism fails—bad consciences and favored temptations follow the hermit into his retreat. Whatever stratagem is adopted, problems are neither escaped nor resolved by shutting our eyes and hoping they go away.

It is in facing the facts—on God's terms—that answers can and will be discovered. This is Qoheleth's consistent message. And the various threads of his argument point in the direction of our need of *wisdom*. Without wisdom we are bound to be thrown back on resources that, in the view of God's Word, are no better than the song or the laughter of fools (7:5-6). But what is wisdom? A most thought-provoking definition of wisdom has been given by Thomas Manton in a sermon he preached on Jesus' words in Matthew 11:19, "wisdom is proved right by her actions." Manton says:

> By wisdom is meant *the doctrine of the gospel*, called elsewhere *the counsel of God*, as appears from the parallel passage in Luke 7:29-30 [KJV], "And all the people that heard him justified God, being baptized with the baptism of John. But the pharisees and lawyers rejected the counsel of God against themselves." The gospel way of salvation is there called the counsel of God, because it is the counsel he gives to men for their good; as here wisdom, because *it is the result of God's eternal wisdom and decrees*. And elsewhere the doctrine of Christ crucified is called

"the wisdom of God;" and again, I Corinthians 2:7 [KJV], "the wisdom of God in a mystery."[2]

The contours of biblical wisdom are all here: it is revealed in the counsel of God (specifically the death of Jesus Christ, but including the inscripturated Word of God); and it results in the transformation of the lives of men and women as the Holy Spirit brings them to faith in Christ. Biblical wisdom stands in stark contrast with the "wisdom of this world"—also called in Scripture "wisdom of words," "the wisdom of the wise," "man's wisdom," and "fleshly wisdom" (I Cor. 3:19; 1:17, 19; 2:4; II Cor. 1:12). This is the wisdom of autonomous secular-humanist man who has declared his independence from God. In principle, it rejects the whole concept of a revealed wisdom from God. Not surprisingly, the Scriptures declare it to be "foolishness with God" (I Cor. 3:19). It is God who is true wisdom and in relation to whom, through personal faith in Christ, wisdom is embraced and exercised.

When Qoheleth speaks of the need of wisdom, it is God's wisdom he has in mind. True wisdom is never divorced from the words and work of God. Qoheleth is a theocentric antiabstractionist. For him, wisdom does not derive from age, intelligence, or experience *in themselves*, but from the interaction of the directive, revealed truth of God and the responsive human mind and heart.

In this perspective, there is no abstract, secularized wisdom that straddles, Colossuslike, the supposed common ground between competing faiths. The secular notion of wisdom is a self-serving myth in which man can by searching find himself to be god,[3] generating his own meaning from the inductive processes of his own mind and experience. If we are truly to "wise up," it is to the Lord that we must we go. The prophetic charge to Israel to measure the claims of mediums and spiritists against God's Word (Isa. 8:19-20) applies not only to our contemporary critique of modern spiritualists and New Age adepts, but also to our response to the conventional wisdom that presently dominates in our culture. That is to say, we must examine, in the light of God's Word, the prevailing scientistic, materialistic humanism that admits no absolutes, no principles, no insights, and no facts outside of the senses and intelligence of autonomous man.

A World Down Side Up (7:15)

The early Christians were dragged before the authorities with the complaint that they had "turned the world upside down" (Acts 17:6, KJV). Unbelievers recognized that the gospel offered a radical challenge to the status quo. Christ came to a world in which the down side was up. Through the witness of his church, he means to reverse that 180 degrees, by bringing people and societies from the dominion of darkness to the kingdom of the Son the Father loves, through redemption and the forgiveness of sins (Col. 1:13).

Trouble is, the down side still seems very much in the ascendant, even after two thousand years of the preaching of the gospel of Christ. Qoheleth, again assuming the mantle of Solomon, observes the disconcerting realities: "a righteous man perishing in his righteousness, and a wicked man living long in his wickedness" (7:15). Echoes of the psalmist's reflections are heard here. He saw, in his time, "a wicked and ruthless man flourishing like a green tree" (Ps. 37:35). But did this prove that God didn't care or was powerless to do anything about it? At first, it did give him problems. "When I tried to understand all this, it was oppressive to me" (Ps. 73:16). What a perfectly understandable response! Paradoxes are bound to pose a problem, because they are, ipso facto, gray contradictions of somebody's cherished black-and-white assumptions. We like things to be cut and dried, either . . . or, black and white. It is tidy, clean, even logical. This is good and that is wrong, is much more appealing than the ethical murkiness of gray and fuzzy assessments of probabilities and possibilities. We like simple answers. They are, on the face of it, more convenient. But is that always the case? Suppose we say, "God is good, therefore he will zap evil!" We are all well aware that there is plenty of evil about and it is not showing signs of dying out! Some use that observation to argue that either God isn't good enough to care or just isn't there at all. Less radically, many Christians feel confused—as did the psalmist—because God does not seem to intervene with the alacrity we feel he ought to. But does it really follow from the doctrine of the goodness of God that he should instantly and forever banish all evil and turn this world into the perfection of heaven?

Does this notion hold water? The more he thought about it, the psalmist was convinced that it didn't. He found the answer in what, to modern ears, must seem an unlikely place—"the sanctuary of God," i.e., the temple (Ps. 73:17). In the temple he was faced with the fact that God *is* and that he has *a plan of redemption* for lost sinners in a perishing world. This resolved—and still resolves—the paradox of a down-side-up world. Why? Because everything about the temple preached God's covenantal commitment to save a people for himself out of *successive generations* of people.[4] This obviously involved *time*—time during which God would call the nations to repent and believe, time in which redemption in Christ would spread to "more and more people" and "from sea to sea and . . . to the ends of the earth" (II Cor. 4:15; Ps. 72:8), and, just as clearly, time for the judgments of God to be applied throughout the same generations (Ps. 73:17-20). God is dealing with us as individuals, generation after generation. And the context of his redemptive work is a sin-wracked world in which he calls people to look to him and be saved. When the psalmist—in this case Asaph—was gripped by this truth, his heart was stilled, he rejoiced in God his Savior, and he committed himself to witness to his sovereign Lord—"I will tell of all your deeds" (Ps. 73:28c; cf. vv. 23-28).

How did everything in the real world—the paradox of the wicked prospering and the righteous suffering, in particular—come together for the psalmist? Through wisdom from God! Only in terms of the light of God's revelation could he make sense of it all. In the light of God's purpose of salvation the real world was intelligible. He was then able to discern the hand of God at work. And this is the precise point Qoheleth is concerned to get across in the rest of the chapter. It takes spiritual wisdom, born of the Spirit of God and informed by the Word of God, to see the world in a balanced perspective and not be unhinged by the often hideous realities that obtrude upon the lives of people and societies. Wising up to God's wisdom is the burden of our Scripture passage.

The Beginning of Wisdom (7:16-18)
Wisdom has been called "the golden mean."[5] The related idea in the field of personal behavior is that of "moderation in all things."

Today we perhaps find this language rather musty. It seems to suggest that the Christian should never take strong and decisive positions. He should be decisively nice and avoid being even slightly dogmatic. By and large, this has indeed been the dominant ethos of mainstream Christianity, certainly with respect to personal ethics. The effect has been to reduce the claims of the Christian faith from a program of radical life-transforming discipleship to Christ to a kind of lace-curtain gentility expressing the prevailing norms of middle-class culture. This is relevant to our understanding of what Qoheleth has to tell us about avoiding "extremes" (7:18), because, if there is one thing that he cannot be accused of, it is being nice and nonconfrontational or undecided in his views. Qoheleth is strong medicine. He does not mince words. And when he talks about avoiding extremes, he is focusing on specific exaggerated sins. He is not advocating a mealy-mouthed moderatism, in which doctrinal and ethical uncertainty is made a virtue and definite, scripturally formed views are dismissed as extreme, immature, and unloving.

God's way is portrayed as being in the center of the picture. It is a way of truth and of divine love for those who walk in it. It is very clearly defined and admits of no obfuscation or evasion. Jesus calls it the "narrow" road (Matt. 7:14). This is the measure of what is extreme. And what Qoheleth here warns against as extreme are paths that deviate from God's path, whether to the right or to the left. Holy moderation is the avoidance of sin; sin is the measure of what is extreme.

What, then, are Qoheleth's guidelines for beginning to be wise? He points out three things: two are cautions and the third a positive and fundamental basis for growth.

Don't Deceive Yourself (7:16)

Becoming self-righteous or imagining yourself to be an intellectual giant is not the same as true wisdom but evidence of a destructive self-centeredness (7:16). The language is ironic. The charge not to be "overrighteous" or "overwise" cannot be a proscription of either personal holiness or the possession of great wisdom. Rather, hypocritical pretension and self-deceit are in view.

It is very easy for people to make a show of what they think is their goodness and for clever people to parade what they think is their wisdom. The only corrective is the Holy Spirit, born-again humility that gives us a true view of who we are before God (Rom. 7:18). Then there will be more humble faith and less playing at religion, more of the heart and less of the externals, more of God and less of self. The first extreme to avoid is that of self-righteousness.

Don't Indulge Yourself (7:17)

The second caution is very startling: "Do not be *overwicked*" (7:17a). It seems to suggest the possibility that moderate wickedness can be part of a good and balanced life! Yet we know from Scripture that God will not look upon sin and that to be guilty of one point of his law is to be guilty of it all (Hab. 1:13; James 2:10). Any wickedness is *over*wickedness with God. We are called to be perfect as he is perfect (I Pet. 1:16). How then can we square Qoheleth with all this bedrock truth? Is Qoheleth not saying exactly what the world wants to believe: Sow your wild oats, cheat a little here and there, but don't go over the score?

The answer is surely that he is saying that there is enough wickedness clinging to our souls without giving ourselves over to it! The context is a discussion of wisdom. Would it be wise to indulge sin? Answer: "Why die before your time?" (7:17b). That extreme is no nearer to wisdom and blessing than the path of the self-righteous.

Where Wisdom Begins (7:18)

Wisdom begins with the fear of God (7:18b; Prov. 1:7). Therefore, "It is good to grasp the one and not let go of the other" (7:18a): in other words, grasp the dangers of self-righteousness and never let go of your convictions about the sinfulness of sin. Significantly, this is the same language used by Jesus in his awesome condemnation of the Pharisees, recorded in Matthew's Gospel. Referring to their attention to tiny details of ritual righteousness and their gross unrighteousness with respect to the central principles of God's law, the Lord said to them, "You should have practiced the latter, without neglecting the former" (Matt. 23:23). Jesus shows that overrighteousness and overwickedness are really two extremes that come together in the same people. The former is a cover for the latter. The true fear of God leads away from such things and is the way of life and joy in fellowship with the Lord.

Being Vulnerable (7:19-22)

If we begin with the fear of God, we must continue with an honest appraisal of our personal weakness. We must be ready to be *vulnerable* before God, men, and ourselves. This has a number of practical implications.

We must first recognize the real strength of wisdom—it makes one wise man "more powerful than ten rulers in a city" (7:19). The wisdom of God is the rightness of God. That is strength. The number and position of those who oppose it only tells us how easy it is for us to be fools.

We must also recognize our need of wisdom. Even the best of people are flawed (7:20). Everyone sins. Weakness is in our nature. We need that powerful input from outside of ourselves which only the wisdom of God can provide.

We must, therefore, admit our personal weakness and, by implication act wisely and generously with respect to the faults of others. Otherwise there will be no end of dispeace and strife. For example, what people say is often unhelpful, if not injurious. It is better not to know everything that people say (7:21-22; James 3:2). You may hear more than you want to hear, more than you need to hear. And if you hear your servant cursing you, you should remember that "many times you yourself have cursed others" (7:22). Learn from the hurtful things you have said of others. How much good did they achieve? What good will it do to hear similar things said of yourself? Qoheleth mentions this to show that wisdom acts like an editor of life's experiences. It selects what is helpful and trashes in advance what would have deleterious effects. Like a good editor, wisdom does not chase the wrong story. It does not eavesdrop. It does not listen in the wrong places. It slanders no one, is "peaceable and considerate," and shows "humility toward all men" (Titus 3:2).

Working at It (7:23-29)

Given a basic faith-commitment (the fear of God) and a vulnerable attitude, how may one grow in wisdom? Qoheleth gives four lines of approach that will lead to a deepening understanding of what is happening in our lives.

Understand Our Own Limitations (7:23-24)

Qoheleth had given a great deal of thought to the meaning of life. He had been "determined to be wise" (7:23a) and had "tested by wisdom" (7:23b) all sorts of problems and solutions—that is, everything discussed thus far in Ecclesiastes. The deeper you sink, the sooner you hit the bottom. "This was beyond me" (7:23c) denotes his unconditional surrender to human finitude and frailty. The human brain is a powerful weapon in the quest for understanding, but even at the level of marshalling simple facts, it is very limited. The body of knowledge is now so vast that the days of the polymath—a brilliant individual, like a Leonardo da Vinci or an Isaac Newton, with an almost comprehensive knowledge of a wide range of subjects—is gone forever. Wisdom has always been more elusive than mere knowledge of facts about the world. Wisdom touches eternity and the mind of God. Bowing before the very concept of God's omniscience (all-knowing-ness), the psalmist declares, "Such knowledge is too wonderful for me, too lofty for me to attain" (Ps. 139:6).

Charles Bridges is so right when he says that "our highest knowledge is but a mere atom, when compared with the unsearchable extent of our ignorance. The more we know of God—his nature (Job 9:7)—his works (Psalm 92:5)—his dispensations (Romans 11:33), the more we are humbled in the sense of our ignorance."[6] This is what Augustine called *"docta ignorantia"*—informed or learned ignorance[7]—the kind of knowledge that is content with its real limitations and able with a quiet spirit to trust a loving Father-God for all that we cannot know.

Understand the Human Problem (7:25)

Again he applies his mind to the human condition. The words, "mind," "understand," "investigate," "search out," "wisdom," "the scheme of things," "stupidity," "wickedness," "madness," and "folly"

portray all the intensity of a great intellect striving to make sense
of a great enigma. It is precisely the stark contrasts in human behavior that pose the conundrum. How can rational man be so irrational? Why does the image bearer of God sometimes stoop to the
most brutalizing and dehumanizing excesses? Why is a world so
full of life disfigured by so much misery and death? And why, more
personally, have I found this out not just by reading the news-
papers and keeping my eyes open, but by doing it myself—by ex-
perimenting with foolishness and self-destructive wickedness?
Qoheleth calls us to reflect upon what we do and why we do. And
we are to measure it against the wisdom that begins with the fear
of God (7:18).

Understand Relationships (7:26-28)

The central strand that runs through the human condition is
the sin factor with "its certain tendency to our misery and ruin."[8]
Because none of us is an island, this expresses itself in our relationships. Perhaps not surprisingly for someone speaking as a latter-
day Solomon, Qoheleth finds sexual relationships the most bitter
of all. In particular, he warns against the predatory seductress who
will surely ensnare the sinner and from whom only "the man who
pleases God" will "escape" (7:26). Given our modern sensitivities to
sexist language, it is important to set these words in their proper
context. Qoheleth is speaking here from personal experience and
he speaks as a man. He was certainly no woman hater (cf. 9:9). He
is not saying that men are not guilty of their own brand of preda-
cious misdemeanors toward women. His observations are simply
from his personal viewpoint. And it is significant that he realizes
his own need of God's power to keep him from sin. He does not
blame the temptress for his own weaknesses. Like Paul, he saw the
need of God-centered self-control (I Cor. 9:7). And in the area of
sex, this is all the more essential because of the power of the emo-
tions involved and the potential for harmful effects on individual,
family, and community life. Broken relationships are often broken
from the start, just because those entering into them do so without
any solid basis. When Qoheleth later talks about the joy of happy
marriage, he clearly sees that arising from a mutual commitment to

marriage as God has planned it—a monogamous, lifelong relationship for partnership, procreation, and, not least, piety.

In assessing men and women in general, he finds very little to encourage him. His poetic statistics for the relative uprightness of men and women cannot be meant to draw any serious comparison between the two. To suggest, as he does, that men are one-tenth of one percent better than women is to deride the very idea! It is equivalent to saying, with the psalmist, "there is no one who does good, not even one" (Ps. 14:3; cf. Rom. 3:10ff.). Like Diogenes, Qoheleth is looking for an honest person, and he is looking in vain. It is a comment on man's need of salvation.

Understand God's Plan for Mankind (7:29)

While Qoheleth's conclusion is that mankind has only itself to blame for its predicament ("but men have gone in search of many schemes" [7:29c]), the truth is that God made us for something better ("God made mankind upright" [7:29b]). Almost cryptically, he hints at a redemptive purpose in God's mind. Why else would he be writing? Is the only reason for mentioning that God made man upright at the beginning to exonerate God from responsibility for man's subsequent regression? Surely not! There is hope, and it is rooted in God's plan for the human race. What does God have in store? Look to him! Listen to his voice! Turn to him in obedience! Please him and serve him! Wise up with the wisdom that God is revealing to his people!

The Goal: The Truly Wise Man (8:1)

Wise people are a treasure. "Who is like the wise man?" (8:1a). Wise people are distinguished by a depth of knowledge and understanding of life and its meaning and purpose. They know "the explanation of things." But this is no mere head knowledge. It is light that shines from the innermost being. The Lord says he "will beautify the meek with salvation" (Ps. 149:4, KJV). True wisdom passes a very practical test: "Wisdom brightens a man's face and changes its hard appearance" (8:1b). That brightness is the light of Christ's righteousness shining forth in a life of practical godliness. Knowing the Lord softens facial features as much as it melts the hardness of the heart. The Christian is a letter to the world, "known and read by everybody" (II Cor. 3:2). Christ, who is the wisdom of God, is read on the faces of those who love him (I Cor. 1:24). Wise up . . . in Christ your personal Savior! Then let your light shine brightly that they may see your good deeds and come to praise your Father in heaven.

Questions for Discussion

1. Do you think it's true that "people may run away from problems but problems never run away from people"? Why don't evasion, escapism, emigration, and eremitism (becoming a hermit) work? Why does God think wisdom is relevant to our life experience?

2. How and why is this world down side up (v. 15; Ps. 37:35)? How does God challenge this situation (Acts 17:6)? In Psalm 73:16-28 what made David revise his estimation of the prosperity of the wicked?

3. Why are we warned about being *over*-righteous, *over*-wise, and *over*-wicked (7:16-17)? Does this mean we can be moderately foolish and sinful (I Pet. 1:16)? How does true wisdom avoid extremes (7:18; Prov. 1:7)?

4. Why is being vulnerable before God, others, and ourselves so much a part of gaining true wisdom (7:19-22)?

5. How can we grow in wisdom? Outline the four steps in 7:23-29.

6. Who is the wise man? How can we identify him (8:1)?

9

RESPECT AUTHORITY!

Please Read Ecclesiastes 8:2-17

> *Obey the king's command, I say, because*
> *you took an oath before God. . . .*
>
> *Whoever obeys his command will*
>   *come to no harm,*
> *and the wise heart will know the*
>   *proper time and procedure.*
>
> *Ecclesiastes 8:2, 5*

The father watched his three-year-old son run around the doctor's waiting room. The toddler paused only to slam the door open and shut . . . and again . . . and again. "Don't do that, or the people in the office will spank you," said his dad (telling a lie). "No they won't," retorted the boy (calling his dad's bluff). And on he went, slamming the door back and forth. "Then I'll spank you," came the weak reply (an obviously idle threat, never acted upon). Turning to the receptionist, he lamented, in the hearing of his little whirling dervish, that the lad was "too smart" for him. "He's all right with other people, but with his Mom and Dad he's the first to tell them to 'Go to hell!' He sure knows when you're bull— — — him!" Then, having provided this foul-mouthed bad example and tacitly abdicated his parental responsibility, he managed to gather his little charge and steer him out of the office.

This story is not made up. It is being repeated in millions of families in the United States, and it is symptomatic of the disintegration of the social fabric of Western post-Christian societies. When we think of the breakdown of authority and order, we naturally associate it with crime and terrorism. We think of it in terms of law

and order and the power—or weakness —of the judicial system of
the state. The rising crime rate is routinely greeted with a plaintive
litany about lenient judges, inadequate penalties, and too few
policemen. The underlying assumption is that the state is weak
and that all the woes of societal breakdown arise from this source.
It is very questionable, however, whether the facts can sustain such
a thesis.

The state is not weak in the sense that it is unwilling to employ
severe measures to achieve its particular goals. It is not lenient
where its own security is threatened. Treason and fraud against
government agencies often draw more severe sentences than
crimes against the person, including murder. What we are seeing, I
believe, is not leniency per se on the part of the judiciary, but a
shift in perspectives and priorities in society as a whole. A transformation has taken place in the way in which authority and respect
for authority are viewed in the West. Lawlessness and lenient sentences arise from a mass decline of the will to be law-abiding—the
decline, if you like, of that mainstay of stable societies, the law-
abiding citizen. This represents the creeping anarchy that cannot
but result from the rejection of the very idea of a law with absolute
standards of right and wrong. The three-year-old in the doctor's
office has no respect for his father's authority because there is no
true authority to respect in his father. The father does not really
know what law is and is therefore incapable of providing his child
with any consistent system of order. He is actually teaching the
child spiritual anarchy. When he does assert some control, it is by
the violence of a foul mouth and episodic, even arbitrary, force.
The essential point is that the basis, in terms of principles, for discerning right from wrong has eroded away. Russ Pulliam, colum-
nist for *The Indianapolis News*, comments on the astonishing fact
that a high school newspaper in Ohio could run a series of articles
on cheating without once indicating that cheating was wrong.
"The problem," says Pulliam, "runs deeper than just adding values
education to the curriculum or learning some standards of right
and wrong. With a few notable exceptions, the world of learning is
dominated by thinkers filled with doubts, not necessarily about
the existence of God—but doubts about the certainty that God

has revealed universal standards of right and wrong to all people. If God has not revealed such standards, then the efforts to teach ethics is doomed from the beginning. It's just one person's opinion against another's."[1] This is moral relativism. What this means in practice is that everyone does – or tries to do – what is right in his own eyes, and the result is lawless behavior throughout every level of society (cf. Judg. 17:6). This is the process we see advancing in Western society today.

From Qoheleth's viewpoint, spiritual and ethical anarchism is but another aspect of the meaninglessness of under-the-sun secularized life. Where there is no God, absolutes cannot exist; relativism rules, and that means that people will do what they can get away with – and define it as good. Yet, precisely because it is the ethics of shifting sand, injustice and frustration are its most prominent fruits. Therefore, in addressing the question as to how this meaninglessness can be rolled back, it is to be expected that God's Word would teach us that we can be happy and enjoy his blessing in a proper respect for authority, both civil and divine. Having told us that we can learn from experience (7:1-14) and grow in wisdom as God's children (7:15-8:1), it is a short step to bring us to the prospect of enjoying the good hand of God in the context of an ordered life (8:2-17). Two main themes attract Qoheleth's attention in this pericope: first is the positive principle that we are called, in the Lord, to be obedient to the civil authorities (8:2), and second is that God will bless his people even under injustice and an oppressive government (8:12).

Obey the King (8:2-4)

At the beginning of every Cub Scout meeting we held up our right hands in salute and recited the "Cub's Promise." This included a solemn undertaking to "do [our] duty to God and the Queen" (we were Scottish Cub Scouts and Queen Elizabeth II was our sovereign). In all the years I was in the Scouting movement, I must have recited that promise hundreds of times, yet that central promise is all that I remember of it. It seemed then, as it still does, a very momentous pledge. It is not a profession of faith in Christ or a commitment to a denominational creed, but it is a politico-religious loyalty oath to the Crown—the monarch being the personification of the British Constitution. The Pledge of Allegiance here in the United States enshrines a similar commitment, although in notably less direct language. The phrase "one Nation under God" envisions the Almighty as more of a spectator to the pledge than the object of the duties pledged, but he is nevertheless the paramount spectator who is sovereign over the nation and is an interested witness to both the affairs of the nation and the sincerity of the allegiance being pledged.

This is precisely the import of Qoheleth's first major proposition. It is that rulers are to be obeyed: "Obey the king's command, I say, because you took an oath before God" (8:2). It seems that there was some kind of pledge of allegiance in ancient Israel. Whatever it was, it is clear that submission to the king was made by a solemn oath before God and it is equally clear that this was, and is, consistent with the teaching of the Word of God. We are, for example, to "fear God, [and] honor the king" (I Pet. 2:17). The Scriptures are explicit on this point. The *locus classicus*, of course, is Romans 13:1-5, where the central principle is laid down that "the authorities that exist have been established by God" (13:1). Because of this, "it is necessary to submit to the authorities, not only because of possible punishment but also because of conscience" (13:5). The *practical* reason—the fear of punishment—is mentioned first, one supposes, because it is the one reason that always comes immediately to everyone's mind. No one ever wants to suffer the punishments of the law! Qoheleth therefore urges a realistic respect and circumspection in dealing with the authorities. Even in obeying the law, it is wise to show respect for its majesty and power. Don't hurry away from the king's presence or stand up for a bad cause (8:3). Take account of the king's power and avoid provoking his displeasure unnecessarily (8:4).

There is, however, a deeper, distinctly *theological* reason for a prudent and respectful submission to authority, namely a conscientious desire to obey God. This is the more profound reason because it gives expression to the true basis for all submission to the authorities. It is not, as we shall see, a case of blind unquestioning obedience of the my-country-right-or-wrong variety. The oath implies that there is a higher allegiance due to God himself. His will is the first and most important consideration in this, as in all aspects of life. At the same time, situations can arise in which obeying God means disobeying the authorities (Acts 4:19; 5:29). There are things to be rendered to Caesar and other things to be rendered to God (Matt. 22:21). But Scripture is clear that within its proper, God-defined sphere, civil government is to be submitted to *out of a desire to follow the Lord faithfully.* The time may come, when, like the apostles, "we must obey God rather than men" (Acts 5:29), but until that moment we are called by God to submit to the powers that be.

Knowing the Proper Time (8:5-7)

God-honoring submission to authority is *never blind obedience.* The state is neither our conscience nor our ultimate sovereign. We are never called by God to a blindly passive and amorally slavish conformity to whatever laws men may decide to impose. We are actually called to an active, analytical, and ethically biblical response, even in the face of potentially threatening consequences. If this is done with wisdom, the danger may be averted and it may even be possible to achieve great things. "The wise heart will know the proper time and procedure" (8:5).

At the best of times this requires patience and an ability to read the signs. This first came home to me in a brush with the police in Turkey. On an overnight train ride across Anatolia, we had dozed off for no more than half an hour and awoke to find our cameras had been stolen from the overhead luggage rack. When we arrived in Uskudar, on the Asian side of the Bosporus from Istanbul, we made a beeline for the police office at the train station. The policeman on duty evidently had us khaki-clad backpackers pegged as a pair of Western hippies (it was the mid-sixties, and we were two newly graduated zoologists on the way home from a holiday/field trip to the Taurus Mountains). He immediately accused us of selling the cameras, and he refused to register our report—which we needed to recover the insurance back in Britain. My friend, Dick, was a deal bolder than I: he didn't take it lying down. He sounded off to that policeman as if the whole of the Royal Navy were off-shore with its guns trained on that grubby little office! But the more he protested, the surlier that policeman became. It was clear that the days of *Pax Britannica* had slipped away! We realized our tactical error and quietly withdrew to the British consulate. Only when a consular official took us to the central police station in Istanbul were we able to come away with the paper we needed.

There is a proper time and correct procedure! There are numerous examples of this in the Bible. Jonathan, for example, chose exactly the right moment to speak to his father Saul about David (I Sam. 19:4-6). Nathan the prophet told David a story about a stolen lamb and then, with impeccable timing, rebuked David for stealing another man's wife (II Sam. 12:1-14). Esther went in to King Ahasuerus in such a way as to effect the salvation of the entire Jewish community in the Persian Empire (Esther 7:2-4).

But why is there "a proper time and procedure for every matter" (8:6a)? Qoheleth's answer is—and it sounds strange to begin with—that no one knows the future (8:7). Why does he say this? Because not knowing the future makes us frustrated—"a man's misery weighs heavily upon him" (8:6b)—and being frustrated causes us to rush in where angels fear to tread! Impatience always tends to make a mess of things. There is only one answer to this problem. Jesus gave it to the disciples when he sent them out to evangelize the Jews: "When they arrest you, do not worry about what to say or how to say it. At that time you will be given what to say, for it will not be you speaking, but the Spirit of your Father speaking through you" (Matt. 10:19-20). This is a promise for all believers. The Holy Spirit will lead his people and instruct them in the spirit of their minds. The right time and procedure will be made plain to those who truly seek the Lord's will with a patient and trusting attitude.

The Limits of Human Authority (8:8)

God-honoring submission to authority does *not* imply *unlimited obedience*. Qoheleth has spoken of the propriety of obedience toward our rulers (8:2-4). He also spoke of the importance of careful procedure in approaching the authorities, especially when some change is desired (8:5-7). Now, just in case we feel that we have no freedom of thought or action in relation to the power of the state, he tells us that it has very real limitations. However wise and respectful we ought to be to kings and politicians, we need not be cowed into servility or craven fear in their presence. They do not have unlimited power. The state is not God, however totalitarian it may be, however godlike its pretensions to regulate the lives of its subjects. These limits are evident in two monolithic facts.

God Reserves Some Powers (8:8a, b)

"No man has power over the wind to contain it" (8:8a). "Wind" (Heb., *ruah*) is better rendered "spirit" in this context.[2] The human spirit is beyond the control of human authority. Likewise, "no one has power over the day of his death" (8:8b). "Ah!" you say, "but kings and dictators have exercised power over the day of the deaths of millions of their victims!" True, but what Qoholeth is getting at is that human authority cannot *prevent* death when that day has come. The day of each person's death proves the finitude of human power. When King Canute set his throne before the rising tide and thereby demonstrated that he could not hold back the ocean's waves, he proved, dramatically and by all accounts deliberately, that he was not to be regarded by his subjects as possessing godlike powers.[3] Is the human spirit any easier to contain than the wind and the waves? Can the power of government prevent minds from thinking their own thoughts? The fact is that the tentacles of the greatest tyrannies have failed to crush the life out of the human spirit, far less thwart the purposes of God. And what of all the confidence that emanates from the corridors of power? And the apparently limitless pretensions of politicians to better the lot of mankind and control human destiny? Who remembers the Locarno Pact between the Great Powers that, in 1925, forever abolished war as a means of solving disputes between nations? Has seventy years of official atheism in the Soviet Union removed Christianity from the face of Mother Russia? History, like the slave at the shoulder of the victor in the Roman Triumph, cries out to the kings of the earth who would be gods, "Remember, you are human!"

God Exercises His Judgment (8:8c, d)

"Wickedness will not release those who practice it" (8:8d). This is as certain as the fact that "no one is discharged in time of war"

(8:8c). The illustration is apt, for it is God, the avenger of wickedness and injustice, who wages war on those who oppress his people. Qoheleth's point is that wickedness—the absolute power that corrupts absolutely—may seem to provide the despotic government with the means to impose its will limitlessly and to offer that government release from the problems it faces. Think of the draconian measures employed in Hitler's "final solution" of the "Jewish problem." Ponder Stalin's slaughter of millions of property-owning peasants, the "kulaks" and Pol Pot's destruction of a third of the entire nation of Cambodia/Kampuchea, all in the name of redemption from capitalist imperialism! And what did the self-styled "king of Africa," Idi Amin Dada, achieve for Uganda by all his brutality but the transformation of the "pearl of Africa," to use Winston Churchill's phrase, into a charnel house? Unrestrained power collapses under its own weight. Evil destroys and self-destructs at one and the same time. But more than that, as E. W. Hengstenberg observes, such apparently irresistible powers "have only importance until God's time and judgement draw nigh."[4] God's power in the exercise of his righteous judgment (3:17) is the ultimate limitation of the ambitions of kings and presidents.

Coping with Injustice (8:9-15)

Abuse of authority is the rule in most of the modern world. Even in nations blessed with the checks and balances of a long tradition of personal freedom and the rule of law, injustice is rife, and the oppressed wage constant battle against those who simply want to lord it over others and take advantage of them. Qoheleth's concern is with the proper response of faith to such a situation. How ought we to respond to the abuse of power and the injustice that follows in its train?

Injustice Is Rife (8:9-12a, 14)

Qoheleth highlights five instances of injustice:

1. Authority is often exercised to the hurt of those whom it is supposed to serve (8:9b). The NIV rendering "to his own hurt" is in error.[5] Self-destruction is not in view—Qoheleth is thinking of the victims. To those at the receiving end, it is always painful to see a

trust abused and those in authority become an enemy rather than a protector. This tests our faith, because it leads us to wonder why the Lord allows it all to happen.

2. The wicked are praised in life and eulogized in death in the very cities where they practiced their injustices (8:10). It is one thing to observe the terms of the ancient maxim, *De mortuis nil nisi bonum* ("Say nothing but what is good of the dead"), but quite another to canonize an utter reprobate as if he were as pure as the driven snow! Injustice at this level also tests faith and tempts us to think that there may be no justice in the universe after all.

3. The sluggish execution of justice is observed to have the effect of encouraging lawlessness in others, as they become persuaded that they may get away with light punishment . . . or even get away scot-free (8:11)! Justice deferred can seem like justice forever denied.

4. The wicked are seen enjoying the benefits of their misdeeds throughout long lives, in the course of which they apparently avoid any penalty for their actions (8:12a). It is almost becoming the custom nowadays for convicted criminals to write best sellers about their naughty lives. This, too, seems manifestly unjust.

5. Often we see a reversal of natural justice—"righteous men who get what the wicked deserve, and wicked men who get what the righteous deserve" (8:14). We sometimes see startling examples of this—none more shocking than the Jews' rejection of Jesus and choice of Barabbas (John 18:40). But more frequently, perhaps, it is an undertone—like the background wash of a water color painting —a general feature of injustices great and small.

Perhaps the only surprising thing about these phenomena is that they were recorded of a society that existed some 2,500 years ago! It takes no imagination to identify similar things going on in modern America. Most of us could illustrate each point from the daily newspaper or even from the lives of people we know. There really is nothing new under the sun! And isn't it intriguing that the abuses Qoheleth pinpoints are grassroot injustices—not the epic evils like mass murder, wars of aggression, and multimillion dollar stock exchange scams? It is not that the spectacular inhumanities of man to man are of lesser account—just that many of us are only touched by them through history books and the media. For the most part, it is the local injustices that materially affect us and wreak their havoc in our real world. Frustration with that neighbor who seems to will his dog to foul everyone's yard but his own; resentment at a local business that first conceals and then defends waste disposal practices that polluted the water supply; anger at the irresponsibility that siphons off tax money into politically motivated projects, while the roads decay and the truly needy are neglected. A climate of oppression can exist because of the "little" things. And it is because these are such ever-present realities in a community or a nation that everything can seem to be meaningless (cf. 8:10, 14).

Faith Has an Answer (8:12b-13, 15)

To man's universal experience of injustice, as exemplified in the above five instances, Qoheleth offers two practical and God-centered answers. These are the answers of faith and are as universal in their applicability as the injustices he mentions are in their capacity to frustrate us.

First, Qoheleth supplies the doctrine: Consider the *destiny of the righteous and the wicked* (8:12b-13). In an echo of Psalm 73, Qoheleth expresses as an article of faith that the prosperity of the wicked is an illusion. Things will not ultimately go well for them, whatever appearances there may be to the contrary. On the other hand, he can say, "I know that it will go better with God-fearing men, who are reverent before God" (8:12b). He *knows* in the sense that he believes with unshakable faith. It is not what he has seen with his eyes in the world. It is what he sees with the eyes of *faith*—faith in what God has revealed, reinforced by his personal experience of God's grace. It is in the nature of faith to look beyond the evidence of the senses. "Faith is being sure of what we hope for and certain of what we do not see" (Heb. 11:1). By faith, the believer knows that God's perfect justice is being worked out. And it is because of his faith in the doctrine of divine justice and the essential goodness of God that he can retain a sense of proportion about the as yet unredressed injustices of wicked people. To know the self-revealing God is to know that his will is being done and that this must issue in the blessing of God's people and the overthrow of injustice and oppression and every other contradiction of the mind and will of God.

Second, the practice follows from the doctrine: The God who is just and good wants his people to *enjoy his good gifts* (8:15). God has *given*. This is the bedrock truth that is to motivate our use of all our gifts. Eat and drink and be glad! Don't let the perplexities of life poison your God-honoring enjoyment of all he has given you in life! "For everything that God has created is good," says Paul, "and nothing is to be rejected if it is received with thanksgiving, because it is consecrated by the word of God and prayer" (I Tim. 4:4-5). Christians should not only be the happiest people in the world, they should be *seen* to be enjoying the good gifts of God! The Christian life is often portrayed as a sad, narrow, restricted, and joyless existence. A world that finds its joys in the pleasures of sin will always want to see it that way, but sometimes we Christians can give the impression of an austere and brooding discontent with life. Perhaps we think it is more pious to be grieved all the time about the state of the world. Or maybe we take a perverse joy in constantly carping about other people's sins. Yet God is clear in wanting the leading motif of our lives to be a redeemed joy, relaxing in the sunshine of his smile and exulting in the assurance of his love. The Christian life is a festival, and like any celebration it is to be filled with joyous exhilaration (I Cor. 5:8)!

The Enigma Remains (8:16-17)

Qoheleth's answers cannot begin to satisfy under-the-sun secularism. The under-the-sun philosophy has no God who brings the wicked to justice and rewards the faithfulness of the righteous. It therefore cannot find any great contentment while perceived grievances are unredressed in this life.

This perhaps explains why we live in a society characterized by an obsessive commitment to litigation and multimillion dollar claims against the slenderest of offenses. It also suggests why, in societies less fertile for such legal maneuvers, the frequently preferred option is that of revolution and the gun. Men without God must have it all now, or it will be gone forever.

In contrast God's people know by faith that they already have what really counts and will really last. They have it right now in their hearts. They see that there can be no ultimate answers in under-the-sun terms, no perfect world through man's best efforts, no fully satisfactory resolution of injustice outside of the complete outworking of God's eternal plans and purposes. It would be dishonest for any Christian to say that he is not troubled by the fact that his Father-God continues, generation after generation, to permit bad things to happen in the world. To trust that God will sort everything out in the end, in his own good time, is a comfort, but it does not remove the heart cry for an end to sorrow and tears (see Rev. 6:9-11). To enjoy the good things that God has given does not cancel out the painful anomalies and inequities so obvious in the global condition of humankind. The enigma remains: even God's people know his blessing and his grace in tension with their as yet unfulfilled desire for the completion of his work of redemption and the full establishment of the final kingdom of Christ.

However much we understand, writes Charles Bridges, "a vast *terra incognita* lies beyond us."[6] The work of understanding must not stop, but the wisdom and knowledge of God is a great deep (Rom. 11:33). It is said that the first lesson taught by the Greek philosopher-mathematician Pythagoras was silence.[7] This was surely a wise echo of the foundational claim of the living God: "Be still, and know that I am God" (Ps. 46:10). Qoheleth expresses the paradox of faith: "Then I saw all that God had done. No one can comprehend what goes on under the sun" (8:17ab). He saw all and consequently could not comprehend! The more he learned, the less he grasped. He bowed in awe before the all-knowing God in realization of his utter dependence upon his Savior!

> When reason fails
>   With all her powers,
> Then faith prevails
>   And love adores.[8] (Isaac Watts)

Questions for Discussion

1. Why are we to respect the proper authorities (8:2-4; see also I Pet. 2:17; Rom. 13:1-5)? Identify the *practical* and the *theological* reasons. Should we ever disobey the authorities?

2. Is this an unquestioning and unvarying obedience (8:5-7; see

also Acts 4:19; 5:29; Matt. 22:21)? What does the Preacher mean by "the proper time and procedure"?

3. Are there limits to human authority (8:8)?

4. What injustices do people often have to face (8:9-15)? Discuss Qoheleth's five examples and his suggestions as to how we may cope with them.

5. Will we ever fully understand what is going on (8:16-17)? What is the relevance of faith to the enigmas of life (Heb. 11:1; Rom. 11:33; Ps. 46:10)?

10
LIVE IN HOPE!
Please Read Ecclesiastes 9:1-10

Anyone who is among the living has hope.
Ecclesiastes 9:4a

*T*hings go better with Coke," claims the famous Coca-Cola ad. Whatever the intrinsic merit of the product, there is one undeniable truth behind this statement, and it is this: People are motivated to spend money by the belief that their purchases will bring them some tangible benefit. All advertising sells hope before we ever buy fulfillment. No one commits himself knowingly to something that has no reward of some kind somewhere along the road. This is a fact of life.

We can all understand this in the world of consumer economics. But is this true of spiritual—specifically, Christian—commitment? Is it perhaps rather crass to think of Christian faith and life in terms of rewards? I think of a prayer I heard frequently at school assemblies in my youth.[1] The central line of thought was that the Christian's reward was in knowing he was doing God's will. We were "to minister and not to be ministered unto; to labor and not to seek for any reward, save that of knowing that we do Thy Will." This sounds so terribly noble and impregnably spiritual. Not for us the earthly returns of the stock market or the bounty hunter; ours is the inward satisfaction of a job well done for God! On reflection, however, this has to beg some questions. What is the place of hope and of reward in the Christian life? Do we look only for inner peace arising from the assurance that we are doing God's will? Is the Christian faith an exclusively existential experience, as implied in the prayer? Does it have tangible rewards now and hereafter? Is a life of Christian hope only a trip—or does it lead somewhere real, eternal, and heavenly?

A young Christian—a sophomore in college—was talking one day with some Christian friends. "You know, when I think about the Christian life . . . well, supposing we die and there actually is nothing in it . . . no heaven, no eternal life, no God even . . . I think it would still be worth living . . . it is a *better* way to live . . . a happier, cleaner, more useful way. . . . Don't you think?" One man—a mature Christian—shook his head, "Man, if there is really nothing in the Christian faith, nothing in the promises of God, then we'd be fools for believing a lie! Why would we bother ourselves with it all? If there is really no God, no heaven, no salvation . . . just death and the end . . . then you might convince yourself the 'Christian life' is nice and makes you happy, but don't pretend that that means anything. You might as well live a life of sin because it would be all the same in the end. It would all be a lie! It is because the promises of God *are* true and because we actually do have a *destiny* in time and eternity in Christ, that our lives have meaning and purpose. We are going somewhere. And we know where we are going because Christ has told us, he leads us, and he will ever be with us until the day he gathers all his people together in glory!" His point was that it is romanticized existentialism to see the fruit of the Christian faith as bound up in our inward spiritual state in this life, however happy we may feel. Such a faith is all journey and no destination. And this, it so happens, is exactly the New Testament view of the subject: "If only for this life we have hope in Christ, we are to be pitied more than all men" (I Cor. 15:19). Paul's point is that because Christ actually, bodily rose from the dead, then in him all believers have an eternal destiny of resurrection life in glory.

But even the assertion of a sure and certain hope of heaven calls forth the criticism that all we really have is pie in the sky, by and by. That may be real but it is not yet ours. Meanwhile, what use is being a believer? What is God doing for us now, if indeed he is so all-powerful to secure our future in this next life of which we are so convinced? The negative, even mocking, tendency of this line of questioning is painfully obvious. It is in the same vein as that which Christ had to endure as he hung on the cross; "If you are the King of the Jews, save yourself" (Luke 23:37). A God who has prepared a heaven for his people ought to be seen to be doing them some good on the earth! The argument may beg some questions, but it strikes an uneasy note in many a believer's heart. It is a fair question. Why do God's people not live out their lives in a glowing corona of success and consistent holiness? The fact is—and Qoheleth saw this in his day—that when it comes to the normal run of life, the righteous and the wicked experience much the same. And sometimes injustices are visited on the righteous, while the wicked get on pretty well (cf. 8:14). What then are the advantages, if any, in being a child of God in this world?

The Paradox of Providence (9:1)

Before answering this, Qoheleth muses on an essential paradox of the believer's life: "So I reflected on all this and concluded that the righteous and the wise and what they do are in God's hands, but no man knows whether love or hate awaits him" (9:1).

First of all, he recognizes that God is in sovereign control of the lives of his people. He holds them *in his hands* (9:1a). We are reminded of the presentation of God's providence in Ecclesiastes 3, except that here, the focus is deeply personalized. It defines the particular grace of God for each believer, one by one. They are known to him by name. His hands surround and guide their every breath. This concept of ever-present divine care is found throughout Scripture. The holding of someone's hand speaks of *love* toward that person. Moses therefore confesses before God, "Surely it is you who love the people; all the holy ones are in your hand" (Deut. 33:3). The holding *up* of another's hand is an act of exaltation, as for example in the proclamation of a champion. God's people are his *prize*, his jewels, even his regalia! "You will be a crown of splendor in the LORD's hand; a royal diadem in the hand of your God" (Isa. 62:3). Scripture also portrays God's hands as unbreakably holding his children and therefore surrounding them with an *everlasting security.* Jesus confirms this when he says of all believers, "I give them eternal life, and they shall never perish; no one can snatch them out of my hand" (John 10:28).

Nevertheless, Qoheleth observes, this does not guarantee an easy and comfortable life, for "no man knows whether love or hate awaits him" (9:1b). In other words, you cannot predict whether people will love you or hate you. God's love toward you does not guarantee that people will be fair to you and treat you well. The world is full of free men and women who freely sin and do so in the face of their personal responsibility and God's revealed will. God upholds believers in this potentially malicious milieu, but he does not promise them moonlight and roses! And no one needs persuading that the real experience of God's people is oftentimes very difficult indeed. Christians are not immune from the ordinary troubles that afflict the human race. We are strangers neither to heartache nor to personal failure.

Given these two facts of Christian life—the all-embracing providential care of God and the common human experience of the vicissitudes of life—what then is the benefit of being a child of God? If our practical experience appears to have no obvious advantages, can it be said that there is any real evidence for our hope? Or is it all a meaningless exercise in self-deceit and wishful thinking?

"We're a' Jock Thamson's Bairns!" (9:2-3)

When a Scotsman wants to emphasize that we human beings are all in the same boat in this fallen world, he says that we are all "Jock Thamson's bairns." Jock Thamson (John Thompson) is the common man and we are his "bairns" (his little children). It is a way of saying to those who have pretensions to being something grand that when all is said and done, "a man's a man for all that" (Robert Burns). If this is too folksy a way of putting it, Paul, quoting Greek poets to Athenian philosophers, pins it down with magisterial simplicity, when he says we are "God's offspring" (Acts 17:28-29).

In practice this translates into the fact, as noted by Qoheleth, that we all share a common destiny, whether good or bad, clean or unclean, churchgoers or not (9:2a). The point is, as Michael Eaton observes, "that the righteous are not visibly favoured by providence, nor the unrighteous visibly rebuked by providence."[2]

The proof of this is that death – the ultimate providence – comes to all of us. This is the great evil under the sun (9:3a). Death is not a normal part of life, like birth and childhood. It is an enemy and an evil. It is the wages of sin (Rom. 6:23). And it comes to all without discrimination or exception (Heb. 9:27).

But why has Qoheleth led us from the idea of common humanity to common experience to death, and finally to sin? Why does sin have to come into the picture? Simply because it is impossible to analyze the human condition and, specifically, the believer's experience in the world, apart from sin, condemnation, and death.[3] The life of lost, unconverted sinners is characterized by "evil" and "madness" that signally affects both their lives and their destiny (9:3b). It is a potentially *lifelong problem* – "there is madness in their hearts while they live." This sin is not a part-time hobby but a matter of the most profound *devotion* – "the hearts of men, moreover, are full of evil." Furthermore, sinners are sinful from the *innermost depths* of their being – "there is madness in their hearts." What this adds up to is a terrifying, but sadly accurate, view of the human condition, apart from spiritual rebirth and conversion to Christ through personal faith in him as Savior. Charles Bridges, with shocking but holy honesty, says that "it is impossible for the sinner to be more dangerously mad than he is, except by growing into greater wickedness."[4] People dread mental illness with all its attendant problems. How much more should they flee from the madness of unbelief in God and unrepentance toward the Lord Jesus Christ! The worst madness in the world is the mind-set and heart commitment that runs from God to enlist with Satan's legion of spiritual terrorists. Sane sinners are in the grip of the most awesome insanity on earth.

While There's Life, There's Hope (9:4-6)

If the picture is as dismal as this, can hope be a practical possibility? If Qoheleth is right – and who can refute him – how can anyone experience hope?

The answer is implicit in Qoheleth's method. Some years ago, a fit young athlete was admitted to Guy's Hospital in London, England, suffering from heart palpitations. So fast was the fibrillation that it was impossible to feel a pulse in the normal way. In fact, he broke the record for the highest heart rate in that hospital. The one thing that had to happen was to get that pulse back down to normal before any permanent damage was done to the heart muscle. How did they do it? They applied massive electric shocks to the chest! And this did indeed do the trick. Our sinful condition is a heart problem as real as but infinitely more serious than palpitations. And we need the shock treatment of God's Word when it tells how dark are our hearts and how great is our danger! But with the shock comes the prospect of new life. Yes, there is hope! And it is to be found in how you respond to the Lord with the life he has given you, right now. The simple fact is that you only need to be alive to have hope! "Anyone who is among the living has hope," for, after all, "even a live dog is better off than a dead lion!" (9:4). Death is the point of no return between time and eternity. You cannot live it over again if you wasted it the first time. And you cannot enjoy life in retrospect. Unlike pay increases, the enjoyment of life cannot be made retroactive to January 1!

The finality of death casts its shadow over present activities and calls for some self-evaluation. "The dead know nothing" (9:5b). This is not to say there is no life after death, but only to emphasize the impossibility of undoing the past from across the great divide. Even the successes and rewards of wickedness in this life can only leave an eternally bitter aftertaste of what is lost forever. The "men of this world whose reward is in this life" (Ps. 17:14) is one of the great themes of Scripture. In the story of the rich man and Lazarus, Jesus has Abraham say to the rich man, who is in hell, "Remember that in your lifetime you received your good things" (Luke 16:25). What ought to have been sought and received, modestly and moderately, as a blessing of God and a means of doing others some good, became for the rich man his summum bonum —his highest good and principal goal—and thus, in turn, became his god. In death, the rich man knows his awful loss, but in Qoheleth's sense he "know[s] nothing," for he cannot cross the eternal chasm between this world and eternity. There is "no further reward and even the memory of them is forgotten" (9:5c).

The living, in contrast, have a great advantage. They "know that they will die" (9:5a)! The sheer austerity of the statement takes one's breath away! We who are alive have hope because (Qoheleth argues) we know that we will die some day! It seems almost trite or even derisive to suggest an idea like this. How can the inevitability of death become an engine of living hope?

The answer is found in the nature of biblical paradox. What seems so contradictory is in fact inseparably related and, in the plan of God, is designed to do us good. On an earlier occasion, Qoheleth told us that "the day of death [is] better than the day of birth" (7:1b). The reason for this, as we saw, was in the paradox that, if we are willing to think seriously about these things, death reaches into our inner-most being in such a way as to profoundly change the pattern of our future lives, whereas birthdays represent backward-looking sentiment that has no power to mold whatever future years God may give us. In other words, we can take the prospect of death, concentrate our minds on where we are now, and redeem the days ahead in devotion to the Lord. Then, as that sublime biblical expositor, Archbishop Robert Leighton, so beautifully expressed it, "Death which cuts the sinews of all other hopes, and turns men out of all other inheritances, alone fulfills this hope, and ends it in fruition; as a messenger sent to bring the children of God home to the possession of their inheritance."[5] So death, the enemy, is defeated by grace. And the first step in that transformation from defeat into victory is to look death squarely in the face *in God's terms* and realize that there is a life to live, in Jesus Christ, that death shall never conquer. This is true hope.

Living in Hope (9:7-10)

As a practical rule of thumb most people probably think "living in hope" is the capacity to put up with a daily life that is boring and unsatisfactory, while looking forward to the better days that will, one hopes, arrive in the future. Hope, to put it another way, is basically a survival technique that makes the frustrations of the present more bearable, even worthwhile. The greater the certainty of that hope becoming reality, the more acceptable the pain of waiting for the ship to come in.

This is undoubtedly and unavoidably an ingredient of all hope, since all deferred rewards cannot but be an incentive to persevere. Very little of any consequence is achieved in this life without some struggle. No investment of pain and toil is voluntarily sustained for long without some hope of surcease and return. And why should it be otherwise? Work, after all, is not an end in itself but a means of providing for our needs and even our comfort. Who would plough and plant if there were no hope at all of a harvest? Surely not anyone with any sense in his head!

Christian hope, in the nature of the case, has this basic underlying character. Moses, for example, "regarded disgrace for the sake of Christ as of greater value than the treasures of Egypt." Why? "Because he was looking ahead to his reward" (Heb. 11:26). Indeed, all the faithful saints mentioned in Hebrews 11 are commended for their faith precisely because they persevered toward the goal of the promised reward. Even so, not one of them actually "received what had been promised" (Heb. 11:39), because these promises pertained to Christ and an era yet to be unfolded. They were, however, not without real blessings in their lives. There are many promises of God besides those which prophesied to the Old Testament believers about the coming of the Lord Jesus Christ and that which promises heaven to us New Testament Christians. But they are all in the nature of rewards, and the incentive of reward, however centered in spiritual things, is not to be despised as an unworthy motivation in the Christian's heart. Such motivation need be no more carnal and self-seeking than the grace that provides the reward of redemption in Christ. It is certainly possible to seek God's blessings with utterly self-centered motives. This is part of the story of human sin, and the Bible is filled with examples of people who tried to gain favor with God through self-centered and self-righteous means—from Cain to Saul and from the Pharisees to Ananias and Sapphira. But to have a holy vision of the glory that God will yet reveal for us and in us, through our Savior, the Lord Jesus Christ, is simply the bedrock of all true Christian hope. With Moses, we rightly look ahead to our reward, and with Paul, we joyously anticipate an eternal glory that will outweigh any present troubles (II Cor. 4:17).

There is, however, in the Christian hope, another dimension of reward that deepens and enriches the daily living of life far in advance of heaven and the eternal reward of unfading glory. Perhaps this distinction is best illustrated from the life of Jesus. John's Gospel records Jesus' "great high priestly prayer" on the last night he spent with the disciples prior to his death on the cross. In that prayer he says to his Father "I have given them [his disciples] the glory that you gave me" (John 17:22). Then, in almost the next breath, he prays, "Father, I want those you have given me to be with me where I am, and to see my glory, the glory you have given me because you loved me before the creation of the world" (John 17:24). Clearly these are two different manifestations of the same glory. The first had already been given to the church on earth; the second awaited them in heaven with Jesus. The latter is the eternal state of glory in the presence of God, while the former refers to the spiritual experience of believers in this life. But what does Jesus have in mind here? What glory did he have that he gave to his disciples? Surely the glory of his holiness and righteousness as the suffering servant of the Lord! And this is the glory of the church after Pentecost—the glory of sharing in Christ's triumph over sin, through a life of commitment to him in lively faith. It is the glory of the paradox that the world sees but cannot quite fathom, namely, that being Christlike means sharing the fellowship of his sufferings and thereby sharing in his redeeming victory (I Pet. 4:13).

The fullness of the Christian gospel was not in Qoheleth's mind as he wrote the Book of Ecclesiastes. But apart from the explicit Christ-centeredness of New Testament teaching on the Christian life and hope, his picture of the way we ought to live breathes precisely the same spirit in which godly hope is to be lived out today by Christians. He addresses the question of how we can live in hope—how hope can raise us above the disappointments and frustrations of life in the act of responding to the *real situations* of life as opposed to merely enduring them until we come to heaven. To live in hope *is* to experience the glory that Jesus gives *now*, while we also wait expectantly for the glory he will give later in heaven when we shall see him as he is (I John 3:2).

Qoheleth identifies four areas of living in which the spirit of hope produces a harvest of joy in the Lord – the joy that works the Lord's glory in us and increases our faith to overflowing.

Contented Living (9:7)

Contentment is God's mandate for our lives. The world, for the most part, derives its contentment *from* things, whereas Christians bring contentment *to* things. True contentment is an act of faith. It is a decision about our attitude based on obedience to God's stated will. God never sanctions discontent, for discontent is the denial of faith, and without faith it is impossible to please God. Qoheleth is emphatic. His word is a command from God: "Go, eat your food with gladness . . ." (9:7a). The gladness comes before the eating, not after it. "Living hope" is the fruit, as Peter puts it, of the "new birth . . . through the resurrection of Jesus Christ from the dead" (I Pet. 1:3). It is "the anchor for the soul, firm and secure" (Heb. 6:19). It is therefore the organizing principle of the believer's attitude to life. That is why, in Christ, we shall be "more than conquerors" (Rom. 8:37). When, in faith, we bring this heart attitude of contentment – which is living hope applied in advance to whatever comes into our horizon – we will not be overwhelmed by the discouragements of the world, the flesh, or Satan himself. A Christian has no reason to complain![6]

And the reason for this is our acceptance by God: "for it is now that God favors what [we] do" (9:7b). Obedience is built upon acceptance, not acceptance upon obedience. We are called to righteous works, not to works-righteousness. We are not trying to persuade God to accept us; we are given the gift of living for him because we are already accepted, through faith in Christ.[7] We can expect blessing with open faces and joyous hearts.

Cheerful Celebration (9:8)

Celebration must flow from the knowledge that God favors what we do. Therefore, it is appropriate for God's people to clothe themselves with a spirit of cheerful praise. "Always be clothed in white, and always anoint your head with oil" (9:8). There is far more here than wearing clean clothes and looking after your complexion! In

Scripture, white clothes are associated with the praise and the glory of God (see Mark 16:5; Matt. 17:2; Rev. 3:4, 5, 18; 19:8). They symbolize not purity—as most people assume—but victory. This was why the great Lutheran preacher, Philipp Jakob Spener (1635-1705) had himself buried in a white coffin! He was expressing his belief in the glorious future of the church of Jesus Christ.[8] The practice of anointing the head with oil was a common feature of celebrations and feasts in the ancient world. This was the "oil of joy" symbolic of the blessing of God (Ps. 45:8; Isa. 61:3). Christians ought to be the happiest people in the world. We have every reason to celebrate. Are we not saved by the Lord Jesus Christ? Do we not have a glorious destiny in Christ our Savior? And if God be for us, who shall be against us?

Companionship (9:9)

Companionship in marriage is to be enjoyed, even sought. "Enjoy life with your wife, whom you love" (9:9a; cf., 4:9-12). The shared life of husband and wife is designed by God to be a community of love and mutual support. The burdens of a meaningless life and meaningless days—i.e., life viewed as short and wracked with uncertainties—are not only shared but counteracted and turned to blessing. "For this is your lot in life" (9:9b) sounds dismal, but the NIV translation is misleading and wrongly conveys a picture of glum resignation. The idea is thoroughly positive: "this is your *portion* in life" tells us that a loving marriage partner is a wonderful gift of God. A portion in Scripture is a share in good things.[9]

Commitment to God's Calling (9:10)

After death, there is no way of doing what we ought to have done before. There is "neither working nor planning nor knowledge nor wisdom" (9:10b). Therefore, redeeming the time and claiming the fruits of the life God has given us requires energetic application (working), practical strategies (planning), informed accomplishment (knowledge), and skillful execution (wisdom). "Whatever your hand finds to do, do it with all your might" (9:10a) allows no room for a flee-the-world mentality. Because this is God's world, God's people have the mandate of heaven to live joyfully, hopefully, and fruitfully as they claim through their work and witness the dominion over the creation that God gave man from the beginning (Gen. 1:28). God's children have work to do and a world to win. And the motivating power for our commitment to life comes from the Savior, who is "Christ in [us], the hope of glory" (Col. 1:27). Christians know where they are going, and they know who is going with them. The English Christian thinker, John Owen, points out that "hope in general" is no more than "an uncertain expectation of a future good which we desire." In contrast, Owen says, the Christian hope, in Jesus Christ, is "a gospel grace" and therefore "an earnest expectation, proceeding from faith, trust and confidence, accompanied by longing desires of enjoyment."[10] For this reason, the uncertainty is removed and a vision of the fruitfulness of discipleship to Christ takes center stage in the mind and motivation of the believer. We live in hope, because Christ, who is the hope of glory, lives in us by the Holy Spirit.

Questions for Discussion

1. If we are "in God's hands," why do we not know whether love or hate waits for us around the corner (9:1)? Do God's people have no security (see John 10:28)?

2. How ought we to respond to our "common destiny" (9:2-3)? Why are sane sinners in the grip of the most fearsome insanity on earth?

3. Discuss the story of the rich man and Lazarus (Luke 16:19-31) and show how it illustrates the point in 9:4-6, that while there is life, there is hope.

4. How are we to "live in hope" (9:7-10)? Identify the four areas of living in which hope produces a harvest of joy in the Lord.

11
REMEMBER YOU ARE HUMAN!

Please Read Ecclesiastes 9:11-10:20

> *As dead flies give perfume a bad smell,*
> *so a little folly outweighs wisdom and honor.*
> *The heart of the wise inclines to the right,*
> *but the heart of the fool to the left.*
> *Even as he walks along the road,*
> *the fool lacks sense*
> *and shows everyone how stupid he is.*
>
> Ecclesiastes 10:1-3

When a triumphant Roman general returned from a successful campaign, he might, if notably successful, be accorded a "Triumph." This was the pinnacle of state and public recognition for a soldier. He and his troops, together with their captives and the spoils of war, marched in procession through the streets of Rome to receive the plaudits of the populace. During the procession the general was accompanied by a slave, who stood at his shoulder and, lest the hero should be tempted to think himself a god, repeated in his ear the words, "Remember you are human!"

We all need to be reminded of our limitations. It was the foolishness of Eve to entertain the lie of the serpent, when he assured her that a bite of the forbidden fruit would open her eyes so that she would be "like God, knowing good and evil" (Gen. 3:5). Modern sinners are too subtle and rationalistic to lay any claims to divinity, but the truth is that to reject the living God is to enthrone the man as if he were God—the ultimate adjudicator of what is good and what is bad. In such circumstances, man is his own god, and because he views himself as the ultimate authority, he has already forgotten the true parameters of human limitation. Instead of wisdom, he generates schemes; for moral absolutes he substitutes relativism and the majority vote; and in place of God's revealed truth, the shifting sand of under-the-sun opinion. There is only one alternative to the worship of God, and that is the idolatry of man, whether expressed through manmade religions or manmade secular philosophies. And such idolatry is the most profound foolishness in the universe (Ps. 14:1; Rom. 1:21-23). And insofar as man rejects God both for who he is and for what he reveals for our blessing, man also rejects his true humanness and pretends to an ultimacy completely beyond his essential creaturehood.

Ecclesiastes lays out for us the consequences of forgetting what it means to be truly human. A thread of delicious irony is woven very deftly through the presentation of this theme. It is the notion that when man sees his humanness exclusively as an under-the-sun (secular, godless) humanism, he actually loses the essential perspective that defines both *who* he is and *what* constitutes his true calling and destiny. Denying the wisdom of God and his relationship to him as the creature to his Creator, he embraces the very opposite—under-the-sun meaninglessness—as the conventional wisdom for the new humanity, independent of God and alone in the universe. Qoheleth is therefore at pains to remind us of our human frailty and our need to depend upon the Lord.

The Limits of Wisdom (9:11-18)

The plumber finished repairing the burst pipe and presented his bill to the doctor's wife. "Forty dollars for a burst pipe!" she expostulated. "My husband doesn't get that much for a consultation." "You have my sympathy, lady," retorted the plumber. "I didn't get forty dollars when I was a doctor either!" We laugh at this situation because it represents the reversal of conventional wisdom. Doctors are supposed to be wealthy and successful. We don't expect them to be out-earned by many other professions or trades. We don't expect them to become plumbers. This illustrates the point that the stereotypical guarantees of success are not always what they are cracked up to be. They may sometimes turn out to be very far removed from reality.

Qoheleth enters some cautions about the limits of wisdom. He has just been speaking of what it means to live in hope. He talked of contentment, celebration, companionship, and commitment (9:7-10). It was a vision for the enjoyment of life as the gift of God. And it was neither fantasy nor wishful thinking but a mandate from God based upon the personal acceptance of each believer by God. God "*favors* what you do" (9:7b). A distinction has to be drawn, however, between God's mandate for our lives and God's providence in our lives. We are given gifts to use, things to do, and promises to claim, all to be lived out in faith, hope, and love, with the joy of the Lord in our hearts. We can expect blessing! But the world into which we go is not always friendly and the life of faith even runs smack into "the gates of hell" (Matt. 16:18). Jesus says it clearly, "In this world you will have trouble" (John 16:33). He also says, in the same breath, not to be afraid because he has overcome the world! As far as our experience of life is concerned, the overcoming is after, not before, the trouble. We must not isolate one aspect of God's promises and ignore the others. We must remember that victory only comes with a battle and somebody else's defeat! The favor of God is not a panacea for the ills of the times. Christians will go on living lives of vibrant faith, victorious hope, and exultant joy in their Savior, but they will still have plenty of obstacles in their way. The key to keeping your balance is never to be caught on the wrong foot. Spiritual balance comes from two feet firmly planted on the Rock that is Jesus Christ (I Cor. 10:4; Matt. 16:18): "On Christ the solid rock I stand, All other ground is sinking sand" (Edward Mote).

Qoheleth makes four points about wisdom to illustrate our need for balanced and realistic expectations in life.

Accomplishments Do Not Guarantee Success (9:11)
Five quick-fire examples spring from the Preacher's pen:

> The *race* is not to the swift
>   or the *battle* to strong,
> nor does *food* come to the wise
>   or *wealth* to the brilliant
>   or *favor* to the learned (9:11b).

The reason is that "time and chance happen to them all" (9:11c). This is just to say that things are taking place out of our sight and beyond our foresight that dramatically reverse our natural expectations. God knows but we do not. Even our wisest preparations can be little better than jumping to false conclusions. Whatever our gift—whether speed, strength, or wisdom—it is a fallacy to put our trust in *it* and forget meanwhile that other factors are involved—not least the sovereign purposes of God. He sees to it that "pride goes before destruction, a haughty spirit before a fall" (Prov. 16:18).

Habakkuk, the Old Testament prophet, complained to the Lord that he let a "wicked foe" succeed in his oppression of the righteous. This successful exploiter of the weak was like a fisherman with his net. He cast his net, gathered up his harvest, and was understandably elated because he could live a life of luxury and enjoy the best that this world could offer. And to what or whom was he thankful for this vile success? "Therefore he sacrifices to his net and burns incense to his dragnet, for by his net he lives in luxury and enjoys the choicest of food" (Hab. 1:16). He trusts in his net—in his own unaided abilities. And he uses them to serve his own selfish and unscrupulous purposes.

What Habakkuk is condemning in the wicked, Qoheleth is gently urging believers to avoid like the plague. Don't trust in your net! Don't think that even the gifts that God has given you guarantee trouble-free progress in life. Don't trust the gift—trust in the Giver! Then you will see the Lord do great things through you.

Ignorance of the Future (9:12)

"Evil times" can "fall unexpectedly" upon us (9:12c). We are incapable of controlling the flow of our own lives, however much we plan and however great our talents may be. All of us expect in practice to get up tomorrow morning and get on with a new day. Individuals and great nations live as if they will go on indefinitely. Qoheleth wrote in the context of a seemingly impregnable Persian Empire, the mightiest power of its day. Who would have believed at that time, that in a short space of years, a few thousand Greeks and their youthful king, Alexander, would sweep it all away forever? Our abilities and our wisdom cannot secure our future from unexpected turns. Our only security is the Lord and his promise never to allow us to be separated from his love. Paul recognized the reality of both sides of the equation—uncertainty about future events and certainty, in the Lord, about future destiny—when he declared his conviction that "neither death nor life, neither angels nor demons, neither the present nor the future, nor any powers, neither height nor depth, nor anything else in creation, will be able to separate us from the love of God that is in Christ Jesus our Lord" (Rom. 8:38-39). We may be human, but there is a God in heaven!

Wisdom Is Frequently Unrecognized (9:13-16)

Qoheleth cites the case of a "poor but wise" man who saved a city when it had been besieged by a powerful enemy. We are not told how he did it, but "he saved the city by his wisdom" and was then promptly forgotten (9:15). And what conclusions ought we to draw from this? First, that wisdom is to be prized as a great gift; but, second, that you had better be prepared for some disappointments. If you expect that being wise, stating the truth, and explaining the obvious will gain you the attention, approval, and influence you feel you should receive, then you just have not reckoned with the way of the real world. You have forgotten that you are living in a fallen world where sin has blinded many hearts and foolishness is legal tender in the marketplace of ideas.

Wisdom Is Very Often Overthrown (9:17-18)

People will listen to "the shouts of a ruler of fools"—the Israelite version of a rabble-rousing local politician—when they should listen to "the quiet words of the wise" (9:17). Noise attracts attention, whether from politicians or preachers. Quietness is unexciting and, for many people, gentle thoughtfulness is associated with wimpishness. In Scripture, quietness is the constant characteristic of the relationship between the Lord and his believing people. "Be still, and know that I am God," says the psalmist (Ps. 46:10). Jesus' ministry was quietly delivered and heard in quietness by his disciples. Jesus did not "quarrel or cry out; no one will hear his voice in the streets" (Matt. 12:19). The Lord is not always quiet, it is true. But when he thunders, it is to dispense his judgments and declare his glory.[1]

The message for you and me is that true wisdom is at a premium—it is better than aircraft carriers and nuclear missiles (9:18a). The truth of this claim, comments Ernest Hengstenberg, "would show itself in the example of the powers of the world if they only lent an ear to its voice, and it will one day be proved in the experience of the nation whose privilege it is to possess wisdom, in the day when, notwithstanding its defenceless impotence it is raised to universal dominion."[2] That nation is, of course, the "holy nation"—the church of the Lord Christ (I Pet. 2:9).

A sinister caveat concludes Qoheleth's discussion of the limitations of wisdom and forms a bridge to the succeeding discussion of folly. However precious wisdom may be, it only takes "one sinner" to destroy "much good" (9:18b). In a fallen world wisdom is always swimming upstream. Sin runs with the current. Sin has all the natural advantages. It doesn't need conversions and changed hearts. Wisdom, on the other hand, needs the actual intervention of the Holy Spirit! This is not to minimize the power of the gospel to change men and women. It is simply to explain why we see sin so rampant in the world (see I Kings 22:52; I Cor. 5:6; 15:33; Heb. 12:15).

Is Qoheleth perhaps too doleful and even destructive in the way he assesses our limitations? Someone might be forgiven for thinking this of him, at least on a first reading. Yet surely no one can say that his observations of the way the world actually is, the way we actually behave, and what the Lord's people actually experience in the world are inaccurate. He speaks for God. He gives the heaven's-eye view of life on earth. And his purpose is that we might live for God. Back of it all, lies a vision of the limitless power of God's grace, which reaches into our lives to transform and sustain us. But we must reckon honestly with our human limitations, if his strength is to be made perfect in our weakness (II Cor. 12:9).

The Heart of Folly (10:1-3)

A sober mind is needed in a crisis if mistakes are not to be made. Foolish actions can do a great deal of damage. Qoheleth therefore takes us to the heart of the matter to provide us with a brief but penetrating review of three of the most basic practical characteristics of human folly.

Folly's Small Beginning (10:1)

A little folly goes a long way. It is like flies in the ointment—"a little . . . outweighs wisdom and honor" (10:1). Perhaps we can still remember the shame we felt at some time in the past when we said or did something, possibly in jest or even with good intentions, only to cause hurt to our friends and cast a shadow over our personal integrity. Personal friendships have dissolved into bitterness over a single silly remark. Many lives have been devastated because of that extra couple of drinks on the way home from the office.

Knowing the potential dangers ought to set us thinking about damage control strategies in advance. This is most immediately applicable to our individual personality traits and known foibles. Quick tempers and quicksilver tongues need training and self-control to head off rash outbursts. The apostle Paul speaks of beating his body and making it his slave—a figurative way of describing the cultivation of personal holiness with its constant need of dying to sin and living in the Holy Spirit (I Cor. 9:27; Rom. 8:13). We need to forearm ourselves against the depredations of our own frailties.

Once that self-discipline is in place, there is still no scope for relaxed vigilance. We must be prepared at all times (I Tim. 4:2); we must watch and pray in case we fall into temptation (Mark 14:38); and we must, like Gideon's soldiers at the brook, be ready for action even as we refresh ourselves (Judg. 7:5-7). It is said that Admiral Sir John Jellicoe was the only man who could have lost World War I in an afternoon.[3] The reason for this was that he commanded Britain's Grand Fleet—the steel wall of battleships that stood between the Kaiser's Germany and its mastery of the seas. Defeat for the Royal Navy would simply have meant the end of the Allied war effort. Every time Jellicoe took his fleet to sea, he knew that it would take just one foolish mistake to deliver the Allied cause into the hands of the Germans. The day of testing finally dawned on May 31, 1916, off Jutland, Denmark. When it was done, Britannia still ruled the waves. Admiral Jellicoe had been prepared. He did not lose the war that day, or any other day, for the Germans never challenged him again. He had gained the victory. Qoheleth is urging believers to prepare for victory rather than court defeat.

Folly Is a Heart-Matter (10:2)

"The heart of the wise inclines to the right, but the heart of the fool to the left" (10:2). In Hebrew, "heart" denotes the innermost nature of a person—what we are, what we really think, what drives us and motivates us. The unmentioned watershed between the two is what the old writers, like the Anglican evangelical Charles Bridges, call "the keeping of the heart with God."[4] In Scripture, the right hand side is connected with blessing and honor (Ps. 16:8; Matt. 25:34, 41). The divergent paths of right and left, therefore, are a figurative way of saying that the wise and the foolish start from different precommitments and will inevitably chart separate courses to radically opposing goals. Qoheleth's point is to impress upon his readers that foolishness should not be shrugged off as tolerable and harmless. It is not "just one of those things" to be accepted as a normal (and okay within limits) part of life. Rather, we ought to be sensitive to the depth of the problem and its far-reaching long-term consequences. The reason there is "no fool like an old fool," is that so many young fools never change their ways!

Folly Will Out (10:3)

Eventually folly is seen for what it is. This is the nearest Qoheleth comes to humor in the whole book: "Even as he walks along the road, the fool lacks sense and shows everyone how stupid he is" (10:3). He is an unfunny comedian. A professional comic is funny because he is a clever caricature of the fool. But the fool is ultimately a tragedy because he cannot see himself as he really is. When he thinks his actions are sound and reasonable, they are in fact evidently deficient. The picture of the fool as a man who cannot even walk along the road without betraying himself is apt. He is like the emperor who had no clothes but blithely paraded before his subjects in the belief that he was dressed in the most magnificent finery!

Folly in Practice and Some Helpful Hints (10:4-20)

The remainder of the chapter is a potpourri of proverbial observations about foolishness and its consequences. All are from daily life, and we are bound to run into them sooner or later. Qoheleth clearly intends that we should spot what not to do, and, although he doesn't come out and say it until the last chapter of his book, he is challenging us to trust in God for wisdom in the face of life's trials. Many practical points are made, in no particular order, and these touch us as personally as they must have the people of Israel two millennia ago.

Evil Arises from Fools in Government (10:4-7)

Only twice in this entire chapter do Qoheleth's rather wistful musings rise to the imperatives of command. Both occasions involve being very careful indeed in the way we deal with the authorities (see 10:4; 10:20). This first case pictures a civil servant who is subjected to the (presumably unjustified) anger of a ruler. He is urged to respond calmly and stay at his post, for "calmness can lay great errors to rest" (10:4). The obverse has been noted by the English poet, George Herbert: "Be calm in arguing; for fierceness makes/ Error a fault, and truth discourtesy."[5]

Qoheleth isn't saying we should all be doormats and let everything go by without a word. But grace and practical wisdom can be allies. After all, it can be dangerous to face up to an angry and powerful superior, even if you are in the right! Why stoke the fire when it is already overheating?

Still worse is a situation where folly and incompetence become entrenched and even rewarded in the corridors of power (10:5-7). In such aggravated circumstances, where the "slaves" ride "on horseback" and "princes go on foot like slaves" (10:7), calmness and loyalty would be severely tested. Bad government breeds discontent and disloyalty and is "an evil" (10:5). Qoheleth offers no further analysis, far less advice, and his silence seems ominous. When we are ruled by fools, we need to know that there is a God who is truly sovereign over his creation and that "the king's heart is in the hand of the LORD; he directs it like a watercourse wherever he pleases" (Prov. 21:1). Remembering our humanity is only meaningful when we remember there is a God.

Vindictiveness Returns Like a Boomerang (10:8)

Dig a pit for somebody and you may fall in yourself! Many a terrorist has been blown up by the bomb he meant for his victims.

Just as God promises that his blessing will follow acts of genuine kindness, so he warns of the destructive consequences of maliciousness (Ps. 7:14-16; Prov. 11:3-6; 12:3; 28:10). Our Lord enunciated the basic principle when, at the time of his arrest in the Garden of Gethsemane, he rebuked Peter for striking one of the high priest's men with his sword: "all who draw the sword will die by the sword" (Matt. 26:52). It was this just principle that was applied in the case of Haman, who attempted an Old Testament holocaust by plotting the extinction of the Jews in the Persian Empire. He failed and was hanged on the gallows he had built for the Jewish leader, Mordecai (Esther 7:10). Similarly, the men who had Daniel thrown into the lions' den were later to die in the jaws of the very same animals (Dan. 24). Sin, like a rubber ball, comes bouncing back before too long! When we remember who we are, as people called to serve God, we will seek first the kingdom of God and his righteousness and repent of the sin that—outside of the grace of Jesus Christ, which cleanses, forgives, and renews—would bring us down to self-destruction.

Thoughtfulness Pays Dividends (10:9-10)

We all know how dangerous some of the most normal things in life can be, and we all have a scar or two from painful encounters with sharp objects and the like. Growing up in Scotland, we ate a lot of fresh fish. We lived three floors up in a tenement above the shop of Jimmy Knott the fishmonger. He was a real "blether"—he talked endlessly and entertainingly with all and sundry, including us young fellows. What amazed me was that, as he talked on and on, he filleted his fish at lightning speed and never seemed to look at what he was doing! Yet that razor sharp knife never seemed to as much as nick a finger! Off came the head . . . the tail . . . the guts . . . the skin . . . and presto, a beautifully symmetrical haddock fillet! Jimmy Knott's dexterous fingers were to me a living parable of the value of lots of good practice. "Skill will bring success" (10:10).

Don't Slack Up! (10:11)

A snake charmer can be a skillful practitioner of his trade, but if he loses concentration and fails to establish control over the snake, the consequences can be very nasty indeed. Slackness can be the death of skill. Ability is like a T-bone steak on the grill—neglect it long enough and it'll all go up in smoke. It is not enough to have talent. A wise man will keep his wits about him. Remembering our humanity, under God, awakens us to a lively and vigilant spirit. "Let us not be like others, who are asleep, but let us be alert and self-controlled . . . ," says Paul. "For God did not appoint us to suffer wrath but to receive salvation through our Lord Jesus Christ" (I Thess. 5:6, 9).

No! They Aren't "Just Words"! (10:12-14)

Nothing reveals more effectively the kind of person we are than the things we say. "Words from a wise man's mouth are gracious, but a fool is consumed by his own lips" (10:12). The contrast is apposite, for it shows that the essential difference between the two is that, whereas the words of the wise *go out* and communicate *grace to others*, the words of the fool *turn inward* and produce a harvest of *self-destruction*. It is important to remember that, in Scripture, a fool is not someone who is dull and unintelligent, but someone who is "wrong-headed" in that "his thinking (and therefore his speaking) refuses to begin with God."[6] From his presuppositions to his philosophy and theology, to his attitudes, actions, and words, everything is pointing in the wrong direction —away from the way of blessing as revealed by God. And the longer he goes on in this way, the deeper he gets into the mire. To begin with, these words are "folly" (10:13)—perhaps something ill-advised or silly, but no big deal considered in isolation. Who, after all, goes through life without saying something foolish? But this is a way of life for the fool. It ends as "wicked madness"—"an irrationality which is morally perverse."[7] He "multiplies words" (10:14a) but has no real basis for any confidence he has in them. He has no knowledge of what the future holds. But when did that ever stop a fool from building castles in the air (10:14b; cf. James 4:13; Luke 12:18-20)? Think, then, about what you are saying—it is not "just words." Remember that "the heart of the righteous weighs its answers, but the mouth of the wicked gushes evil" (Prov. 15:28).

"A Fool's Work Wearies Him" (10:15)

When it comes to actions and particularly the consistency and competency required to do productive work, the fool is also found wanting. As with his words, so also with his deeds. He has no inner guidance system. He therefore "does not know the way to town" (10:15b). Plan, goals, and stick-to-itiveness are missing. He may be talkative enough and have endless energy to embark on new schemes, but for all that he is gripped by what Michael Eaton trenchantly defines as "a moral and intellectual laziness which leads to a stumbling (2:14), fumbling (10:2), crumbling (10:18) life."[8] He is a biblical sluggard. If he is energetic, it is not for the right things, and what George Grant has called "his moral catatonia"—i.e., "wasteful and irresponsible behavior"—will eventually "drive him over the edge of responsibility, prosperity, and sanity."[9] This is a word to the wise.

Exercise Practical Political Wisdom (10:16-20)

Qoheleth returns once more to the problem of irresponsible and incompetent rulers, the theme first taken up in verses 4-7. The bones are virtually identical, although the flesh is somewhat fuller of form. What earlier was described as "an evil" is now intensified to a prophetic declaration of an imminent curse. "Woe to you, O land whose king was a servant . . ." (10:16; see Isa. 3:1-5). The contrast between this and the blessing of a land whose king "is of noble birth" serves to emphasize the former nation's predicament even more darkly (10:17). The indicator of the fitness or unfitness of the two monarchs respectively is the way they eat! The prince who feasts in the morning shows his lack of interest in governing his realm. He obviously wants to live a luxurious life, untrammeled by any necessity to work and exercise responsibility. On the other hand, the good king eats "at the proper time"—for strength and not debauchery.

The incompetence of the foolish is not rewarded with a lightning bolt of divine judgment, but with the steady decay of life's infrastructure. Just as the fool is "consumed by his own lips [i.e. words]" (10:12b), so his irresponsible actions cannibalize the very fabric of his existence. He consumes without producing! "If a man is lazy, the rafters sag; if his hands are idle, the house leaks" (10:18). And that is the way with governments and nations, as much as it is for individuals. The self-serving attitude appears to be summed up in 10:19—the debauched rulers declare their manifesto even as they feast on the legalized pillage extracted from their misgoverned and oppressed subjects: "A feast is made for laughter, and wine makes life merry, but money is the answer for everything." Food, wine, and money are all there is for such people. This is the meaning of life! This is the goal of the voluptuary, the summum bonum of the under-the-sun "good life." Eat, drink, and be merry . . . for there is no real tomorrow!

Qoheleth assumes that this will be an ongoing fact of life. His parting counsel is to chart a calm and careful course in relation to the authorities and the big money interests. Don't let them get to you so that you start being foolish and therefore bring unnecessary troubles upon yourself. Keep your own counsel. Be circumspect in your thoughts. Don't even curse the rich in the privacy of your bedroom, because "a bird of the air may carry your words" (10:20). It should be clear from the general thrust of Ecclesiastes that Qoheleth cannot be advising us to abandon all principles just so that we can survive. The context is a discussion of foolishness, and he is simply advocating not doing anything foolish. Martyrdom may come soon enough. And if it comes, let it be for good, God-honoring reasons. The badmouthing of even a tyrant is not an example of the kind of righteousness for which Christians might be persecuted. Picking a fight is not the same as standing for the truth. Qoheleth is urging a quiet wisdom that thinks before it acts and trusts the Lord at every point along the way.

A young lad was going off for a summer job on board a ship plying the Great Lakes. His father had been a merchant seaman before he had become a pastor, and he was conscious of the dangers and temptations of life on the ocean wave. So he gave him a few words of advice. They were few, maybe, but very well chosen: "Son, keep your eyes open, keep your head down, keep your nose clean, and read the Book of Proverbs again and again!" That is, in essence, what God is saying to us through his servant Qoheleth.

Questions for Discussion

1. Why do we need to be reminded of our limitations?
2. Discuss the four limits of wisdom in 9:11-18.

   a. Why are gifts and accomplishments often a snare (9:11)?
   b. Do we really know the future (9:12)?
   c. Is wisdom always recognized for what it is (9:13-16)?
   d. What can happen to wisdom in this world (9:17-18)? What does this suggest about the secular-humanist trust in education to solve the world's problems?

3. Identify the three basic characteristics of human folly in 10:1-3.
4. Review the seven practical points made about folly and wisdom in 10:4-22.

   a. Is "government" always good (10:4-7)?
   b. What about taking the law into your own hands (10:8)?
   c. Is practice not just drudgery (10:9-10)?
   d. Can we never slack off a little bit (10:11)?
   e. Is anything "just words" (10:12-14)?
   f. Can we be too serious about work (10:15)?
   g. Discuss practical political wisdom in action (10:16-22).

PART FOUR
DECISIONS

12
INVEST IN LIFE!
Please Read Ecclesiastes 11:1-10

Cast your bread upon the waters,
  for after many days you will find it again.

Ecclesiastes 11:1

One of the advantages of an invitation to be a guest preacher on one of the small islands off the west coast of Scotland is that the sail on the ferry offers a time of leisurely contemplation in beautiful scenery with lots of wonderfully fresh sea air. On one such occasion—it was a lovely fall day—I noticed that a number of passengers on the promenade deck were throwing pieces of their sandwiches into the water. The text, "Cast your bread upon the waters," instantly came to my mind. It was obvious, however, that this bread was not going to come back "after many days." Much of it was scooped up by the sea gulls even before it hit the sea! Even so, it struck me that in a sense the bread did return to those who threw it over the side. The return was to see the skill, the sheer poetry of motion, of the gulls as they wheeled and swooped around the ship. We enjoyed their enjoyment! We enjoyed the beauty of God's creatures.

There is probably a more literal basis than this for Qoheleth's expression. The time for sowing seed in the Nile delta in the years before controlled irrigation was to wait until the annual inundation receded and then, as the waters went down, to cast the seed onto the water. It would disappear into the soil then being deposited. But, in due course, it germinated and produced a rich harvest. The "bread" in the form of seed[1] must be hidden in the soil in the expectation of the later return of next year's "daily bread."

The central idea is that of faith-commitment of one's resources toward a future of productivity and blessing. Commerce and business also provide a model that illustrates this point. It takes "bread" (in the modern idiom, a reference to money or capital) to make an investment in a new business. And it takes a degree of trust to venture that capital into the uncertain seas of the commercial world.

Qoheleth is concerned with the meaning and direction of life. He began by considering the secular, under-the-sun life — life lived without any regard to God and eternity — and found it to be meaningless. In this, he echoed the despair expressed by those who saw no way out of the tragedies and anomalies of their existence. He agreed with those who found the under-the-sun life inherently meaningless. He agreed that death is a wall the secularist concept of meaning cannot climb. Through ten chapters, Qoheleth exhumed the corpse of humanism (this-world-only, futureless-beyond-the-grave, godless secularism in all its forms) and with relentless logic proved it to be really dead. He has shown us that the industrious inventiveness of self-proclaimed autonomous man to carve meaning for himself from life on planet Earth is little more than the twitchings and spasms of spiritual death. Interwoven throughout his exposition of meaninglessness is an emergent tapestry of rising hope that points to God's alternatives to man's prevailing predicament. The last two chapters of Ecclesiastes call for decisions to be God's disciples and to live in faith for him. The writer's tone changes from the somber to the triumphant, from a darkling pessimism to a luminous hope, rising to a ringing crescendo: "Fear God and keep his commandments, for this is the whole duty of man" (12:13).

Ecclesiastes 11 challenges us to invest in life with a vigorous holy boldness and with a joyous and expectant spirit. Living for the Lord *is* the good life. It is *the* happy life, for it rests securely upon the salvation God has wrought for all who will love him.

Living Boldly, by Faith (11:1-6)

Life is essentially a faith venture (11:1). Casting your bread upon the waters is not an option, but a divine imperative. It is also the only life that has God's promise of his sustaining love and enabling power every step of the way. God's promise is the energizing concept that lifts his commands from the category of the daunting task to the realm of glorious prospect. Why? Because, as Charles Bridges has written, "Faith in the promise gives life to the precept."[2] God's commands, his precepts, are bound to be a great burden where there is no faith. Speaking of his unconverted pre-Christian life, the apostle Paul testified that when the precepts of God came into his ken, "sin sprang to life and I died" (Rom. 7:9). The very holiness of God's law highlighted his spiritual opposition to God, and he himself became more aware of his sinful state. Without faith, God's law came to teach him the sinfulness of sin (Rom. 7:13). After Paul had been converted to Christ, he did not cease to have struggles with sin (Rom. 7:12-25), but he knew that he was free from its guilt and condemnation, "because through Christ Jesus the law of the Spirit of life set me free from the law of sin and death" (Rom. 8:1). His new life in Christ meant that he had a new nature and his ongoing life experience of faith in Christ enabled him to receive God's commands for what they are—the Lord's powerful prescription for spiritual heath and happiness! Faith sees the goal and is drawn toward it in the personal assurance that God is faithful to his promises. Once cast upon the waters of life, the "bread" is subject to God's promise that "after many days" we will "find it again" (11:1).

The Life of Faith Must Be Lived with Commitment (11:2-5)

Bold enthusiasm marks the believer's investment in his discipleship to the Lord. To "give portions to seven, yes to eight" (11:2) indicates the measure of effort. "Seven" is symbolic of completeness. "Eight" goes one step further—it means giving 114 percent! The Lord Jesus Christ rose from the dead on the first day of the week—that is, on the *eighth day*. That is why Sunday is the "Lord's Day"—the day of resurrection from the dead and of new life in Christ. It is symbolic of the New Testament age of gospel light and blessing, because Christ has brought in the "eighth day" of new creation.[3] Giving a portion to "eight" represents the kind of wholeheartedness that comes from a spiritual liveliness born in the heart by the Spirit of God. New life cannot but overflow (Ps. 23:5). Life lives liveliness. Life expands outward, by its very nature.

But commitment doesn't just happen. It can be dampened or fired up; it can be encouraged or inhibited. Why be wholeheartedly committed, when the world is going to be a mess whatever we do? The under-the-sun mentality can easily home in on God's men and women and tempt them to a watered-down attitude to the life and calling God has given them. Why live life with holy gusto? Why venture for the Lord? Two reasons are suggested by Qoheleth:

First, *time and events wait for no one* (11:3-4). Clouds full of water pour out rain; trees lie as they have fallen. We don't control these things, and so it is simply no use waiting for the ideal time or the more convenient season. If you put off living life as you ought to live it, you may find it has slipped away altogether. If the farmer sat around watching the wind and the clouds, he would neither plant nor reap. To be sure, the rain blesses the ground and gives us our food; the fallen tree provides heat for the home—the blessing of God is dropping upon the earth. But that happens in his good time and according to his providence. Our responsibility is to get on with living by faith in the world as we find it. We are to trust the Lord to do his work. It is, after all, beyond our control anyway! Urgency and aggressive faith are called for and are, indeed, the channel into which God has promised to pour his blessings. Procrastination is, therefore, not only the thief of time—it is a predator upon the goodness God would give to us, were we to live committed lives for him; it is the destroyer of lives that would be filled with joy were they to receive the Lord by faith and walk in his way.

Second, *you don't need to understand how God works* in order to find blessing in faithfulness to him (11:5). Ignorance of God's workings is not removed by having faith. The unspoken implication is that faith in God is precisely how we can not only live with our ignorance of the secret work of God in the world, by actually find blessing in the process: "Faith," says Michael Eaton, "flourishes *in* the mystery of providence, it does not abolish it."[4] "How often do we afflict and torment ourselves by our own restless thoughts," asks John Flavel, "when there is no real cause or ground for so doing?" Answering his own question, Flavel explains, "How great and sure a means have the saints ever found it to their own peace, to commit all doubtful outcomes . . . to the Lord, and devolve all their cares upon Him! 'Commit thy works unto the Lord and thy thoughts shall be established' (Prov. 16:3). By works he means any doubtful, intricate, perplexing business, about which our thoughts are racked and tortured. *Roll all these upon the Lord by faith, leave them with Him."*[5]

Get on with the Job (11:6)

Faith in Christ does not relieve anyone of hard work; it only makes it possible to get on with the job in a joyful spirit that expects God's blessing, whatever the immediate outcome may be. Eric Liddell, the great Christian athlete who was the hero of the Oscar-winning movie, *Chariots of Fire*, was knocked off the track while running in an international 440-yard race in Stoke, England, on June 14, 1923. He refused to give up. Twenty yards down when he got back to his feet, he burned up the rain-soaked track to finish first —only to fall off the track again, this time in victorious exhaustion![6]

Qoheleth's counsel is to "sow your seed in the morning, and at evening let not your hands be idle" (11:6a). Get busy! Redeem the time! Diversify your work investment by using morning and evening, even for different goals. The more doubts you have about the general situation, the more diligent you should be to get to work for the Lord in every aspect of life. If the times seem meaningless, *you* are called by God to bring meaning to them! If you "sow for yourselves righteousness," then you will "reap the fruit of [God's] unfailing love" (Hos. 10:12). God has promised that "at the proper time we will reap a harvest if we do not give up" (Gal. 6:9). Paul's encouragement to Timothy the preacher—"be prepared in season and out of season" (II Tim. 4:2)—has its application to us all. Especially at times when we don't feel like putting in the effort ("out of season"), we should be most ceaselessly active in living life for the Lord.

The reason for such driving diligence is precisely because "you do not know which will succeed, whether this [sowing seed] or that [your evening work], or whether both will do equally well (11:6b). The point is a positive one, not a counsel of despair. We may not know the future, but God does. Our job is to work in faith and leave the rest to God. And that is where we can have a confidence that reinforces our commitment and uplifts our hearts. Our confidence is not, please note, in some mystical assurance of success in all we do; it is rather a confidence in the Lord himself and an assurance, by faith, that whatever happens, there will be a blessing in it for us. "Those who sow in tears will reap with songs of joy. He who goes out weeping, carrying seed to sow, will return with songs of joy, carrying sheaves with him" (Ps. 126:5-6).

Living Joyfully (11:7-10)

Christians are not called to be pious drudges. Faith is often thought of in relation to troubles: faith overcomes; faith is triumphant; faith shines from the ashes of affliction. . . . All this is true. But faith also smiles. Joy and faith are the two sides of a gold coin. They glisten in inseparable beauty. So inseparably that it must be said that a joyless Christian is an utter self-contradiction. You cannot be joy*less* in the Lord if you are *in* the Lord at all. Of course life has its ebbs and flows and its ups and downs. But it is precisely in these shifts of joy and sorrow, exultation and discouragement, that we discover all the more preciously just what the joy of the Lord means. No challenge to faith can be complete without a call to rejoice in the Lord. It was not for nothing that Paul exhorted the Philippian Christians: "Rejoice in the Lord always. I will say it again: Rejoice!" (Phil. 4:4).

Life Is Meant to Be Joyful (11:7-8)

One of the most joyful people I ever met was an old Irish lady, long since gone to be with her Lord, who had been afflicted with crippling arthritis almost all her life. She knew she had it, when as a sixteen-year-old, she took the emigrant ship from her native land for a new life in America. Over half a century later, now a widow with a middle-aged retarded son, she lived in a small Iowa town. By that time she was bedridden, her limbs twisted beyond any apparent usefulness, her life restricted by pain, immobility, and concern for her disabled son. The pastor, with whom I was a summer intern, prepared me for the shock of her crippling deformities, but he could never have enabled me to anticipate the sheer Christian joy radiating from that wonderful woman. Sitting at her window, a pen somehow held in her shriveled hand, she was writing letters of encouragement to a network of Christian friends throughout the country. She was truly a fellow worker with God! Her conversation was full of life and bespoke a well-informed interest in the work of the Lord in the community and beyond. Above all, she was full of Christian joy and, notwithstanding her constant experience of pain and discomfort, appeared to be utterly devoid of self-pity. Her body was in ruins, but her eyes shone brightly with gospel light. She was a living testimony to the truth that a life of joy does not depend on favorable circumstances and physical well-being, but on the life of God in the soul. That joy arises from knowing the Lord Jesus Christ as a loving Savior: it is the joy of being saved by his free grace.

First, life, rightly understood and prayerfully lived, is a *joy in itself*: "Light is sweet, and it pleases the eyes to see the sun" (11:7). Life is, as Ernest W. Hengstenberg put it, "a good thing; and when a gloomy and depressing mood gets the upper hand . . . it is the task of the word of God to impress upon [us] this truth."[7] All the misery of sin in the world can neither obscure this fact nor deny the experience of it to the people of God. Perhaps with a twinkle in his eye, Qoheleth asks the under-the-sun skeptics if it is not pleasing to the eye "to see the sun." His point is surely that the creation declares the glory of God and that it is a contradiction of reality to assert that there is nothing but the sun under which to live. The joy inherent in sunlight—that which makes it "sweet"—is something that speaks of God. And that voice has to be suppressed by those who do not wish to know anything of "the Maker of all things" (11:5). Qoheleth's gentle barb calls the doubters and the depressed to look to the Source of the light. In gospel terms we are reminded that the "true light" is none other than the Lord Jesus Christ (John 1:9; 8:12).

Second, this joy lasts a *lifetime* (11:8). "It's great to see the way the kids enjoy themselves . . . no responsibilities," said the woman to her friend as they walked past the playground. "Lord knows, it'll all be over soon enough!" For many people, joy and responsibility don't mix. Children and young adults have fun, but not people with families to look after and certainly not the old and infirm.

The joy that many so wistfully yearn for is the preresponsible life they once knew as children.

Yet God holds out the prospect of lifelong—and long life—blessing (Pss. 23:6; 128:5-6). "However many years a man may live, let him enjoy them all" (11:8a). If this was a powerful reality for Old Testament believers, how much more so it must be for New Testament Christians. Christ has brought life and immortality to light (II Tim. 1:10). In him, there is joy enough for a whole lifetime.

Third, *realistic* reflection upon the "days of darkness" that will come into our lives ought to be stimulus to living life to the full now (11:8b). Again, the under-the-sun perspective leaves its imprint on Qoheleth's exhortation: "Everything to come is meaningless" (11:8c). This is his way of saying "You only have one life to live!" Everything in this (under-the-sun) life is futile, and "fundamentally unreliable."[8] He is not saying anything about either divine judgment or the world to come. He is keeping a narrow focus on this life and the motives and direction that we are to bring to it. We are to live and enjoy *now* the life God has given because it is good to do so. And, since it will soon be over, those with good sense will make the most of it. "Why waste it," he might have said, "even if there is a heaven to come?" A person who refuses to live for the Lord now is not likely to live with him in glory. *Now* is the time to respond in faith to the gifts of God!

Christian joy is the real thing because it is realistic about the nature of life and death, of time and eternity, and of the holy God and sinful humanity. That realism is rooted in the revelation and redemption of God in Jesus Christ. To be saved by Christ is to know his joy—"joy unspeakable and full of glory" (I Pet. 1:8, KJV). Claim that joy! Follow the Lord Jesus Christ.

Practical Joy Is Part and Parcel of the Life of Faith (11:9-10)

The biblical message is always addressed to the human capacity to make choices. We are called to believe in God, to obey his will, to repent of sins, and to choose righteousness. Responsibility and the exercise of mind and will pervade the Scriptures as they do our daily lives. Perhaps surprisingly, the Bible sees joy and happiness as falling within the spectrum of volition. Enjoying life—in a biblical context, for the world's idea of *la dolce vita* is very definitely not in view—is a mandate for believers. We are to choose to live joyously! It does not just happen to us but is produced by the life of faith. This becomes clear as Qoheleth unfolds three fresh points as he concludes his challenge for us to invest in life.

First, "Be happy, young man, *while you are young*" (11:9a) is not an invitation to sow wild oats and party into the wee hours night after night! All of that comes naturally enough and is the dead end of under-the-sun fun and frolic, rather than the joy that pours from the fountain of eternal life. Qoheleth's positive purpose is for youth to exploit its natural advantages and make a maturely happy start to life—in other words, to develop to the full the gifts God has given at a time when freshness and vigor can be most productive. A misspent youth sounds like fun when told as a joke, but it is usually the precursor of a misspent life . . . period. Rather, be seeking true joy in all you do. All that has already been said in Ecclesiastes is packed into Qoheleth's plea; all that he will say in chapter 12 will drive it home for all who have an ear to hear.

Second, it is the *joy of the heart*—the innermost being of a person —that is to be cultivated: "let your heart give you joy in the days of your youth" (11:9b). Says Hengstenberg, "Cheerfulness . . . is not merely permitted: it is commanded, and represented as an essential element of piety."[9] This is the cheerfulness of heart renewed by the Spirit of God (Prov. 14:30; 15:13) not the perversity of a heart of unbelief (Num. 15:39; Jer. 17:9). When we are right with God in our hearts, then we are on track for true joy.

Third, that track is not, however, defined by the movements of our hearts and eyes. The *righteousness of God* is the standard and the ground of true joy (11:9c). Joy is controlled by the awareness of God's judgment,[10] controlled in the sense that it is nurtured and developed—not restricted, as many assume. God is not a killjoy; he is the only source of lasting joy. "Joy was created to dance with goodness, not alone."[11]

The kind of joy you seek now will go a long way to determining what fruit will be produced in later life. An old term for the down side of wasted youth is *after-wretchedness*—the sad ruination of middle and later life that resulted from earlier follies.

Perhaps the opposite ought to be called *after-joy*—the joy that grows by God's grace in Jesus Christ after a sinner is saved and at whatever age he is saved. Qoheleth wants that blessing to begin early in people's lives. Therefore, he calls us to remove the obstacles to a fruitful and happy life. "Banish anxiety" and "cast off . . . troubles," for "youth and vigor are meaningless" (11:10). The under-the-sun motif appears again, for he seems to be warning against not only the pitfalls of sin in the heart and in the flesh, but also the false trust in youth and vigor that is so common in this world. "Youth and vigor" as an abstraction—a golden age of life—is dangerously meaningless. The cult of youthfulness is a broken reed. Peter Pan is as much of a myth as Tinkerbelle. Youth is a quickly passing phase. It can be a time of joy—in the Lord. But under-the-sun youth is a secular mirage that must crumble into joyless regret as advancing time erodes the porcelain finish of the beauty shop and opens up the fissures of irreversible decay. To trust in such youth is to trust in the illusions of the make-up artist. It is to embalm an abstraction and imagine it to be reality.

Invest in life! Cast your bread upon the waters of your times! Qoheleth challenges us to pour our hearts into a faith-response to God's gift of life. It only remains for him to face us with the final challenge—to come to know our Creator as our personal Savior and Lord. And that is the subject of his final chapter.

Questions for Discussion

1. Why is "casting your bread upon the water" an act of faith (11:1)?

2. What kind of commitment does life take (11:2-6)? Why is it an urgent matter? Why is it not necessary to understand how God works in order for us to be faithful?

3. Is life supposed to be sad and miserably difficult (11:7-8)?

4. How is joy to be obtained in practice (11:9-10)? Discuss the purpose of God for youth and some of the pitfalls of youthfulness that is not dedicated to the Lord.

13

REMEMBER YOUR CREATOR!
Please Read Ecclesiastes 12:1-14

> Remember your Creator
> in the days of your youth,
> before the days of trouble come
> and the years approach when you will say,
> "I find no pleasure in them."
>
> *Ecclesiastes 12:1*

The purpose of Ecclesiastes, says J. I. Packer, is to lead a "young believer into true wisdom, and to keep him from falling into the 'York signal-box' mistake."[1] But what on earth, you ask, is a "York signal-box" mistake? What does a signal box in York, England, have to do with the wisdom of God? Packer's answer is "Not very much!" and that is just the thrust of his illustration. He imagines standing on a platform in the train station in York. The trains come and go, this way and that, and if you stay around long enough you begin to understand the pattern of train movements. If, however, you go up to the signal box between platforms 7 and 8, you find an electronic display of all the track within five miles on either side, together with moving, flashing lights indicating the positions and directions of all the railway traffic in the area. "Now," you say to yourself, "I *really* know what is going on. I have a higher knowledge of the rail system than the fellow on the platform!"

Packer's point is that some Christians think of the wisdom of God, and their experience of knowing God, according to this model. They feel they ought to be like the man in the signal box; that to have the wisdom of God is to be able to "discern the real

purpose of everything that happen[s] to them" and to be clear at
"every moment how God was making all things work together for
good."² But the mistake is "to equate wisdom with wide knowledge," whereas, what we need to learn is that "the real basis of
wisdom is a frank acknowledgement that this world's course is
enigmatic, that much of what happens is quite inexplicable to us,
and that most occurrences 'under-the-sun' bear no outward sign of
a rational, moral God ordering them at all."³ God does not let
Christians in on his secret councils; we are still on the platform
with everybody else. The difference is that God's people have been
given a faith that is real and a realism that is faithful. Even our
ignorance is turned into grace, for it produces genuine humility
and a dependence upon God's goodness in his unseen purposes.
God's way of wisdom is not some mystical divining of his secret
will. It is the way of personal commitment and lively faith whereby
we can "trust Him and rejoice in Him, even when we cannot discern his path."⁴

The final chapter is the climax of Qoheleth's appeal. He calls for
decision and commitment. And the heart of that commitment is
not the anticipation of comprehensive inside information about
God's plans and providence; neither is it the expectation of a happy
life unencumbered by the problems that drop into everybody else's
horizon; it is the remembering of God for who he is—the Creator-
God who has made us and placed us in the real world, to the end
that we would be his people in thought, word, and deed. We are
called to "fear God and keep his commandments, for this is the
whole duty of man" (12:13). This is the subject of the climactic challenge of Ecclesiastes.

Remember (12:1)

Remembering things can be a real problem sometimes. A pastor
I know—a particularly gifted preacher who has a masterly command of language—told me that ever since the day he forgot the
Lord's Prayer in the middle of leading his congregation in its recita-
tion, he has never gone into the pulpit without a written copy as
back-up for his memory! A momentary mental lapse can suddenly
produce a blank in the most deeply entrenched of memories!

Biblical forgetting is, however, a horse of an entirely different color. Forgetting God was the great failing of God's people in the Old Testament period (Deut. 32:18; Isa. 17:10; 51:13). Indeed, "all the nations that forget God" fall under the cloud of his righteous anger (Ps. 9:17). And this is no mere mental lapse, but an attitude of heart. It is a *commitment* to forget the Lord, by laying his word and his will to one side. Forgetting the Lord is the other side of living for self. It is part of the Christless, unconverted lifestyle; the instinctive revulsion from the light and impulsion toward the darkness; the unwillingness to receive the things that come from the Spirit of God; the rejection of the knowledge of God and the willing acceptance of what the Lord has declared to be sin (John 3:19; I Cor. 2:14; Rom. 1:28, 32).

Remembering the Lord is, likewise, a good deal more than merely sparing him a thought. When the Lord's people were exiled in Babylon, they confessed their faith-remembrance of God in the most profound language of personal devotion. "If I forget you, O Jerusalem, may my right hand forget its skill. May my tongue cling to the roof of my mouth if I do not remember you, if I do not consider Jerusalem my highest joy" (Ps. 137:5-6). At the heart of this longing for Jerusalem is not the place itself, but the person of the living God, who has made an everlasting covenant with his people, that they would be his adopted children and he their heavenly Father. In him there is life, and apart from him there is nothing. To forget him is to be in the state of spiritual death. To remember him is to know life and to have it abundantly. Jerusalem is the fountain of his free grace because there, in the temple, God was present with his people and making provision for their redemption. And yet all this only pointed to Jesus Christ, who was both temple and sacrifice, both great high priest and blood of atonement, both mediator and sin-bearer on behalf of his people. To long for Jerusalem was to long for all that it represented: for salvation, yes, but all the more for union and communion with the only Savior of sinners. His heart renewed by the transforming action of the Holy Spirit, his life turned around through radical repentance and faith in Christ as the only possible Savior from sin, the believer cannot but be powerfully drawn to remember all that the Lord has done in pouring out undeserved goodness upon him. The believer remembers because he loves: "I love the LORD, for he heard my voice; he heard my cry for mercy. Because he turned his ear to me, I will call on him as long as I live. . . . The LORD is gracious and righteous; our God is full of compassion. The LORD protects the simplehearted; when I was in great need, he saved me" (Ps. 116:1-2, 5-6).

What is precious to a believer must become as precious to the person who as yet has not trusted in the Lord. Qoheleth was speaking to the community of God's covenant, Israel. They knew the message of God's Word, even if they were largely ignoring it's claims. But that is just the point! The thrust of Qoheleth's words is directed to the *unbelief* among God's erstwhile people. It therefore strikes toward the need of all human beings, whether they hear God's Word for the first—or the umpteenth—time. Those who are oppressed by the meaninglessness of life under the sun and see the emptiness of their lives need desperately to remember the only one who can redeem such lostness and fill up the caverns of our despair with his everlasting love!

Qoheleth outlines the three basic motives for remembering the Lord.

You Owe It to Your Creator! (12:1a)

Remember your Creator! The Hebrew *boreka* ("Creator") is a plural form, no doubt echoing the language of Genesis 1:26—"Let *us* make man in *our* image, in *our* likeness"—an indication of the greatness of God's majesty, as Michael Eaton has suggested,[5] but also, surely, an intimation of the three-in-one glory of God the Father, Son, and Holy Spirit. The connection is then made—to be sure, only in the light of New Testament hindsight—between the first creation of man as the image bearer of God and the new creation in God's only-begotten Son, the Lord Jesus Christ, of all who will believe on him in this world.

The point is that God is entitled to be remembered by those whom he has made. He has the exclusive rights to your worship, service, and discipleship! The potter has power over the clay. Not only can you not rightly talk back to God, but you are under an unbreakable obligation to confess him as Lord (Rom. 9:20-21)! You *owe* this to our Creator. You have no right to forget him and go your own way!

You Owe It to Yourself . . . Now (12:1b)

Remember the Lord "in the days of your youth" (12:1b). Some people think that youth is a time for enjoying an almost deliberate irresponsibility. It is taken for granted that young people will sow their wild oats. The only trouble with this is the crop failure that follows afterward! We reap as we sow, and wasted youth may be no better than a jolly fun-filled foretaste of a miserable middle age. When Israel journeyed through the Sinai desert en route for Canaan, they were promised their food, in the form of manna they could collect each day (except the Sabbath) (Exod. 16:4-5, 19-23). The manna did not, however, collect itself: the Lord's people had to get up early and gather it in. They had to collect it before it rotted. Laziness was bad for manna! Youth is like this: if you want a fruitful life (manna), then "let the manna be gathered early in the day."[6] Start young! Look at the barren sadness of many in middle and old age, and ask yourself what you are building for your future now. You will reap later what you sow now—either for good or for ill. Your potential calls you into God's future for your life. Now is the time to begin to realize that potential for your blessing. Your youth is prime time in God's eyes: a time for responsibility, for learning the things that are really important, for molding God-honoring patterns of life; a time for sowing in righteousness in the Lord and experiencing the fruit that Jesus spoke of in the parable of the sower—"a hundred, sixty or thirty times what was sown" (Matt. 13:23). God wants the energy, liveliness, imagination, freshness, and eager expectancy of youth to spread the light of the good news of Christ into every nook and cranny of the next generation as it takes its place in the forefront of societal and cultural development. You owe it to yourself, under God, to take his outstretched hand and, in dependence upon his grace, to realize the fullness of the calling to which he has called you in the gospel of Jesus Christ. Should you not want God's best for your life?

You Owe It to Your Future (12:1c)

Commit yourself to the Lord "before the days of trouble come and the years approach when you will say, 'I find no pleasure in them'" (12:1c). Again, there are echoes here of the Genesis account of human origins—not creation itself, but rather the fall of man into sin and its terrible consequences. Because of sin, we all return to the dust (Gen. 3:19). Like some black-draped Victorian hearse from a Gothic horror story, Death is preceded by footmen called Infirmity and Old Age, whose appearance is a foretaste of the end that must come soon. Qoheleth's intention is not to titillate our morbid fantasies, still less to plunge us into a gloomy frame of mind, but rather to encourage us to anticipate the future and its trials realistically and be in the spiritual condition to face them head-on and win. Summer is the time to prepare for winter—and old age is our physical winter. It can also be a devastating spiritual winter if our hearts are unprepared. Charles Bridges pinpoints the issue: "Old age, with all its train and retinue of weakness and infirmities, will come. But if it *bends your back*, do not keep your sins to *break it*."[7] Life does *not* get any easier. And it is no more than cruel mockery to tell people in the twilight of life, "Pack up your troubles in your old kit-bag and smile, smile, smile," when what is really needed is the solid bedrock of unshakable faith in a personal Savior. As the outward crumbles away, the inner person needs more than a party hat and the illusion of youth and beauty!

The apostle Paul opens up God's answer for us in II Corinthians 4:16-6:2. This passage is required reading for a proper understanding of Ecclesiastes 12. Paul could see the decline of his physical faculties. Outwardly he was "wasting away." There was no use denying it—our bodies are declining assets. But, says Paul "we do not lose heart." Why? Because "inwardly we are being renewed day by day" (4:16). His eyes were fixed on the unseen eternal glory he was receiving in Jesus Christ, rather than on his very visible aches, pains, and aging. In a ringing affirmation of the truth that really counts, Paul declares, "Now we know that if the earthly tent we live in is destroyed, we have a building from God, an eternal house in heaven, not built by human hands" (5:1). The Christian prepares for the future by living out of the future; he lives each day in terms of the unfolding toward him of God's perfect purpose for his future. Faith and confidence go hand in hand. And the Christian owes it to the future to which God is calling him to live *now* for his Father-God the life of the kingdom of heaven, on this side of eternity!

Reflect (12:2-7)

The thought that years will come when we will say, "I find no pleasure in them" (12:1), is as disturbing as it is unappealing. The Dutch pastor-theologian, Cornelis Gilhuis relates how, while visiting a parishioner who had just turned eighty-five, the venerable old man suddenly said to him, "Above my life I could now write the words: 'No more.'" His wife and friends were dead. His house, health, and hearing were gone. He lived in an aged people's home, and so his freedom was restricted. He couldn't walk very well, anyway. And his memory was slipping too. So much he had known and enjoyed was . . . no more. Eventually he too would be . . . no more.[8] A. E. Housman contemplated this dismal reality from the non-Christian perspective in his poem, "Ho Everyone That Thirsteth," a poem in which, with melancholy resignation, he expresses his lack of faith in the gospel of Jesus Christ (notice his pointed allusions to Isaiah 55:1, John 7:37, and Ecclesiastes 12:5):

Ho, everyone that thirsteth
  And hath the price to give,
Come to the stolen waters,
  Drink and your soul shall live.

Come to the stolen waters
  And leap the guarded pale,
And pull the flower in season
  Before desire shall fail.

It shall not last forever,
  No more than earth and skies;
But he that drinks in season
  Shall live before he dies.

June suns, you cannot store them
  to warm the winter's cold,
The lad that hopes for heaven
  Shall fill his mouth with mould.[9]

This is exactly what Qoheleth reflects upon in the highly poetic language of chapter 12. Through the successive phases of the advance of sorrows, the decline of physical capacities, and death itself, the author takes us to the threshold of decision—the urgency of rejecting the meaninglessness of a death-wish society by remembering the Lord of life. The poetic wistfulness with which he explores the facts while masking something of their harshness is a lesson in itself. This is how to preach the good news through breaking the bad news! Cast in figurative language, the bad news is raised from the baldly horrific, earthy facts of decay and death to an altogether higher plane. Qoheleth's elevated language takes us from the cold slab of the mortuary to the quietness of the secret place of meditation, prayer, and the worship of God. We are brought to the loftier consideration that what is lost through physical decline is not some mere phase, or the perception of a phase, in a normal under-the-sun cycle of human existence that grinds on, only to end with a dull thud as "another one bites the dust!" Rather, the author's transition from the merely prosaic into the poetic commands our thoughtful reflection and suggests that there is something better than decline and death. Let us rather see this life, warts and all, as God's chosen arena in which he is working to change our lives and bring spiritual fruitfulness even against the background of physical incapacity. God is saying that the inevitable need not be the ultimate! Now, in youth, and later, in old age, God will produce in all his worshiping people nothing less than the beauty of his holiness—new life redeemed from death by his free grace in his own dear Son, Jesus Christ!

Reflect on Advancing Sorrows (12:2)

The sun, light, moon, and stars grow dark. Rain ceases, only for clouds to return. Real life is a darkling landscape. Sorrows multiply and hearts grow heavier. Gray days make for furrowed brows. The point is that if anyone is to be encouraged and cheered in his old age, that spiritual uplift will have to come from *outside* his personal resources. The perfect illustration for me is the weather of my Scottish homeland. If you can see the hills, it's going to rain; if you can't see the hills, it *is* raining! If warm sunshine is what lifts your heart, there's no use looking for it in Scotland! You have to look for joy in some other direction. Old age is a bit like Scottish weather: there are many rainy days. And joy will vanish with the sun, if it is not rooted in the Lord through a living faith. Remember your Creator.

Reflect on Declining Faculties (12:3-5e)

The proof that the clock cannot be turned back is found in everything we take for granted when we are young:

- The "keepers of the house" are the hands and arms that shake and lose their strength where once they worked indefatigably (v. 3a).
- The "strong men" are the legs that are now bent and pad along the street with shortened stride and unsteady gait (v. 3b).
- The "grinders" are the teeth long lost to dentures and the painful bite of wasted gums (v. 3c).
- Those "looking through the windows" are the eyes, now dimmed, in spite of glasses, so that reading and even general vision offer little pleasure (v. 3d).
- The "doors to the street" are the ears that hear no more with the clarity of earlier days (v. 4a).
- The "sound of the grinding" is a voice, once strong, that has faded to a whisper (v. 4b).
- To "rise up at the sound of the birds" while "all their songs grow faint" is a reference to the light sleep and early waking of the aged, without the consolation of being able to enjoy the dawn chorus of the singing birds (v. 4c).
- Being "afraid of heights" is that loss of a sure foot and steady balance that makes stairs a trial to the old (v. 5a).
- The "dangers in the street" can range from children on bikes to fast cars and muggers who prey on the infirm. The great world outside holds threats that once never crossed a man's mind (v. 5b).
- The blossoming of the "almond tree" is hair turning grey and then white—beautiful in itself, but only for a moment—for, just as the petals drop within a few days, so the greying of the hair marks the fleeting passage of our life (v. 5c).
- The "grasshopper drags himself along" conjures up the image of a late fall day, with a tired old grasshopper—a survivor of

the summer—crawling slowly across our doorstep, his joints too stiff to give free movement to his legs, his muscle too cold and atrophied to speed him on his weary way (v. 5d).

• Then "desire no longer stirred": the general appetite for life, for food, for anything in the spectrum of experience, recedes, and no vitamins or drugs can rekindle the former fires of youthful *joie de vivre* (v. 5e).[10]

And then comes death.

Reflect on Death (12:5f)

"Then man goes to his eternal home and the mourners go about the streets." Nothing is said here of eternity or life after death. The "eternal home" is simply the grave. The central idea is that this life, once over, is gone forever—there is no return, no reincarnation, no revivification by cryonic technology.[11] Life is a one-way trip to eternity. Mention of mourners bathes the scene in unutterable sadness. Dying is a palpable outrage. It is the violation of something that is good in its very nature—the gift of life. Indeed, the Hebrew text reads, "Man *is going* to his eternal home": the participle [Heb., *holekh*] underlines the ongoing nature of the process.[12] We are dying while we live.

Where, in this, can meaning be found? Reflect . . . and "remember him" (12:6).

Now Is the Time to Remember (12:6-7)

Qoheleth pictures for us a golden lamp bowl suspended on a silver chain and a pitcher at a well raised and lowered by a wheel. Such things decay: the light goes out, the pitcher can draw water no more. The time to use them to the full is now! And so it is with life itself. Like silver and gold, like water from a well, life is precious and time is a gift of grace to be invested for a harvest of fulfillment and of service under God.

Soon your "dust returns to the ground it came from, and the spirit returns to God who gave it" (12:7). Why were you given life? To bring glory to the Lord by living as his image bearer in your life on earth. How are you living your life? And when he calls your spirit into his presence, what will your testimony be as to that life?

For whom are you living? What are your goals? Who is your god? Where are you going? The time for decision is *now*—the unuttered implication of Qoheleth's word is that a mistake now may be a mistake forever! "Remember him—before . . . before . . ." (12:6).

Respond (12:8-14)

Qoheleth has turned full circle. He returns to his first words: " 'Meaningless! Meaningless!' says the Teacher. 'Everything is meaningless!' " (12:8; cf. 1:1). Like every good preacher, he concludes with his text! It is his way of saying to us, How have I treated my subject? Have I spoken to your heart? Have I illuminated the problem? Have I pointed to the solution? Have you thought it through with me? Are you ready to respond?

You Have Been Told the Truth! (12:9-10)

Qoheleth declares that all he has said is "upright and true" (12:10). He has exposed the true meaninglessness of under-the-sun secularism. He has exercised all the skill and wisdom at his command. He knows he is wise, a good communicator, a wordsmith of proverbs, and a minister of truth. Yet for all the authority with which he speaks, there is almost a pleading tone in the way he appeals to his readers. It has been no academic exercise, but an explanation of the issues of life and death, of meaning and of emptiness, of the realities of time and eternity. It has been a *Word from God!*

Don't Accept Any Substitutes! (12:11-12)

Because the source is the "one Shepherd"—the same Shepherd as in Psalm 23, the Lord—it is a fully sufficient analysis of the situation. The warning against adding other men's words and becoming bogged down in the study of the books and discourses that flow endlessly from scholars underlines the uniqueness of the Word of God.

"Here is the conclusion of the matter . . ." (12:13-14)

The Lord and his Word are the twin focal points of the entire book: "Fear God and keep his commandments, for this is the whole duty of man" (12:13). This rather stark statement, to which is added an ominous intimation of the final judgment of God on everything, whether good or evil (12:14), comes as something of a cold shock. And yet it is the whole point! Outside of God and a loving reverence for him and his revealed will, there really can only be meaninglessness! The full revelation of the New Testament now clothes this truth with the evangelical warmth of the gospel of Christ. The apostle John tells New Testament believers: "Dear friends, if our hearts do not condemn us, we have confidence before God and receive from him anything we ask, because we obey his commands and do what pleases him. *And this is his command: to believe in the name of his Son, Jesus Christ, and to love one another as he has commanded us.* Those who obey his commands live in him, and he in them. And this is how we know that he lives in us: We know it by the Spirit he gave us" (I John 3:21-24). God has revealed himself to us in all his fullness as the Three-in-One, full of love and grace; the Father-God who is love and is to be worshiped in holy fear; the incarnate Son, the Lord Jesus Christ, the mediator who has died in our place to bear our sins; and the Holy Spirit, who since Pentecost has ministered in the hearts of God's people with transforming power.

A Time for Personal Commitment

On May 20, 1962, a seventeen-year-old lad joined his pals from the high school Scripture Union group for a day trip to Galashiels, a small town in the southern uplands of Scotland that march along the English border. The business of that beautiful spring day was a five-a-side soccer tournament followed by a picnic and an evening gospel rally. Hundreds of kids gathered from all over the southeast of Scotland for this annual event. The soccer was pretty ferocious that afternoon, and it was a weary young man who settled into his seat at the meeting, his mind reverberating with the chagrin of a narrow defeat in the quarterfinal and wondering if he could really be bothered with a sermon on a Saturday night. But you never know, he said to himself, the preacher might bring a good message.

The preacher was the Rev. Mr. Gordon, a Baptist minister from over the border in Newcastle-upon-Tyne. He opened his Bible and read from the Book of Ecclesiastes, chapter 12. As he thundered out the message of that text, line upon line and precept upon precept —always pointing to its thrust in the light of the New Testament fullness of the gospel of Jesus Christ—that teenage audience slid forward to the edge of the hard wooden benches of the Volunteer Hall. As the fleeting gift of youth was set in the context of a short life and a long eternity, the tiredness of limb and mind fled from that seventeen-year-old. He began to hold his breath as the issues of life and death coursed through his head with relentless impetus. He saw, as never before, how life was a gift so easily wasted, how even that day he had been more interested in the soccer than in the Savior, with whom he had always assumed himself to be right and faithful; he saw, with awesome reality, that he was *neither* right with God *nor* committed to his Son, as he had lightly imagined from childhood. He felt suspended between life and death, between self and Christ, between his sins and the Savior; and he knew he was being drawn inexorably to the moment of decision— he would have to choose on that day whom he would serve!

Going home that night, he watched the cat's-eyes along the central median of the road, sparkling in the headlights of the bus. Ahead of them, the road wound through unseen darkness to his home in Edinburgh. The lights seemed, however, to chart a new path for a new life in Jesus Christ. Life would never be the same again. Christ had come and saved him to be his disciple. Christ had brought him by his free grace to "remember" his Creator "in the days of his youth." Christ, he saw, was the only true meaning in an otherwise lost and meaningless under-the-sun world. And Christ had died on that cross so long ago to bring redemption to the likes of him!

I was that young lad. More than a quarter century on, I can surely say that my life has never been the same again. In middle life, youth is becoming a memory even if old age still seems far off. But throughout the passages of life, the Lord Jesus Christ has been the unchanging Savior and the ever-faithful Friend. He is the meaning of our life! He is Immanuel—"God-with-us"—and in him we can have life and have it abundantly! Then we declare with a full heart, "Since my youth, O God, you have taught me, and to this day I declare your marvelous deeds" (Ps. 71:17).

This is the "good life"—the life that the Lord is giving to all who trust in him.

Questions for Discussion

1. Define "forgetting" as it is used in Deuteronomy 32:18; Isaiah 17:10; and 51:13, and contrast it with what it means to "remember" the Lord (see Ps. 137:5-6).

2. Why are we to remember the Lord (12:1)?

3. Is it morbid to reflect on old age and death (12:2-8)? List the details of this passage and tell why they encourage us to remember the Lord.

4. What response is the Lord looking for from each one of us (12:8-14)? What kind of life does he have in store for those who heed his call?

NOTES

Preface

1. Malcom Muggeridge has pinpointed this with his characteristic blend of wit and acerbity in an illuminating essay, "The True Crisis of Our Time," in Geoffrey Barlow, ed., *Vintage Muggeridge* (Grand Rapids: Eerdmans, 1985). He says that "in the gadarene bias apparent in all our policies and projects . . . we are confronted, not with a whole series of crises and problems, but with one crisis amounting to a death wish, an urge to self-destruction seeping into every aspect of our way of life, especially our values, our beliefs, our aspirations, how we see the past and our hopes for the future" (p. 101).

2. Francis A. Schaeffer, *Death in the City* (London: Inter-Varsity, 1969), p. 20.

3. General Millan Astray uttered these astonishing words in Seville, on August 15, 1936. The Spanish Civil War was raging and the general, who had one leg, one arm, one eye, and only a few fingers on his remaining hand, was completely carried away by his own rhetoric—not uninfluenced, perhaps, by his own remarkable survival from the rigors of his profession. See Hugh Thomas, *The Spanish Civil War* (New York: Harper and Row, 1963), pp. 271-72.

4. Alan Richardson, *Christian Apologetics* (London: SCM, 1963), p. 29.

5. Michael Eaton, *Ecclesiastes*, Tyndale Old Testament Commentaries (Leicester: Inter-Varsity, 1983), p. 47.

Chapter 1: What's the Use?

1. Shelley's fictional king, Ozymandius, was the historical Rameses II. His "shattered visage" is in remarkably good shape and on display in the British Museum, London. See F. Kermode and J. Hollander, *The Oxford Anthology of English Literature*, vol. 2 (London: Oxford University Press, 1973), p. 414.

2. The identity of the "Teacher" (Heb. *Qoheleth*) is one of the great conundrums of biblical interpretation. A careful examination of the evidence suggests that the author has melded materials of his own and others in the form of a narrative of the sayings of the "Teacher," who appears to be identified with Solomon, although the latter is never named (1:12; 12:9). There are indications that Qoheleth, as we shall call him in this book, is a personification of Solomonic-style wisdom. It is altogether likely that material of Solomonic authorship was incorporated in the text. (See Herbert C. Leupold, *Exposition of Ecclesiastes* [Grand Rapids: Baker, 1972 (1952)], pp. 8-17; and Michael Eaton, *Ecclesiastes*, Tyndale Old Testament Commentaries [Leicester: Inter-Varsity, 1983], pp. 21-24, for excellent discussions of the issues involved.)

3. Ecclesiastes is now generally regarded as contemporaneous with Malachi, with a postexilic provenance and purpose. The conditions in Solomon's time (see I Kings 4:20, 24) do not mesh with the Preacher's picture of the sad state of Israel. See Leupold, *Ecclesiastes*, p. 12.

4. R. Laird Harris et al., *Theological Wordbook of the Old Testament*, vol. 1 (Chicago: Moody, 1980), pp. 204-5.

5. Douglas R. Groothuis, *Unmasking the New Age* (Downers Grove, Ill.: Inter-Varsity, 1986), pp. 52-55. Groothuis shows how the New Age mysticism is a "cosmic humanism" in which all meaning is found in "the One" as man absorbs God's functions and creation becomes a mystical continuum of existence. When the Creator-creature distinction is obliterated, the creature becomes his own god and is the source of his own ultimate meaning. The facts of his existence, however, are an embarrassing reminder, from time to time, of his true creaturehood. The gnawing awareness of futility can never quite be drowned out, however loud the protestation of man's new independence of God.

6. Erich Maria Remarque, *All Quiet on the Western Front* (New York: Grosset and Dunlap, 1929), p. 278. This classic antiwar novel speaks, of course, of the experience of the soldier in the trenches of World War I. The theme, however, is a statement of meaning in a secular world. Paul Baumer, the ill-fated hero, is modern man, stripped of the delusions of childhood (and, by implication, of religion). "I am young," he says, "I am twenty years old; yet I know nothing of life but despair, death, fear and fatuous superficiality cast over an abyss of sorrow" (see pp. 270ff.).

7. Davin Seay, *Stairway to Heaven* (New York: Ballantine, 1986), p. 171. This is an illuminating survey of "the spiritual roots of rock 'n' roll from the King and Little Richard to Prince and Amy Grant."

Chapter 2: Life's Dead Ends

1. Michael Eaton (*Ecclesiastes*, Tyndale Old Testament Commentaries [Leicester: Inter-Varsity, 1983], pp. 21-24) provides a luminous discussion of this device by which the Teacher speaks as if he were a second Solomon.

2. Derek Kidner, *A Time to Mourn, and a Time to Dance* (Leicester: Inter-Varsity, 1976), p. 29.

3. Hymn 637 in *The Church Hymnary* (London: Oxford University Press, 1930), p. 777.

4. Herbert C. Leupold, *Exposition of Ecclesiastes* (Grand Rapids: Baker, 1972 [1952]), p. 56.

5. Robert Ingram, "Multiplying by Zero," in *Tabletalk*, vol. 11, no. 4 (August 1987), p. 6.

6. Gordon H. Clark, *From Thales to Dewey—A History of Philosophy* (Grand Rapids: Baker, 1980 [1957]), p. 151. The founder of the Cyrenaics was Aristippus of Cyrene (435-366 B.C.). Epicurus of Samos (341-270 B.C.) founded the school that bore his name.

7. Francis Nigel Lee, *A Christian Introduction to the History of Philosophy* (Nutley, N.J.: Craig Press, 1969), p. 88.

8. Eaton, *Ecclesiastes*, p. 65.

9. The moderate use of wine is a recurring thought in the Wisdom literature (Eccles. 9:9; Prov. 31:6-7). There is no suggestion that excessive drinking—or, say (in the modern idiom), the use of drugs—is an aid to thinking and the development of human potential in some mind-altering way.

10. In 1811 John Knill of St. Ives in England built a pyramid like a church steeple inscribed with the text, "I know that my Redeemer liveth" (Job 19:25). After his death he left an endowment and directions that every five years, ten young girls in white should dance around the "folly" and sing the one hundredth psalm ("All people that on earth do dwell") in his memory. This is observed in St. Ives to this day, to the evident pleasure of locals and tourists alike. England, particularly, abounds in such cultural curiosities.

11. Kidner, *A Time*, p. 32.

Chapter 3: Who's in Charge?

1. William E. Henley, "Invictus," in *A Treasury of the World's Best Loved Poems* (New York: Avanel Books, 1980), p. 122.

2. Ernest W. Hengstenberg, *A Commentary on Ecclesiastes* (Minneapolis: James and Klock, 1977 [1869]), p. 92, quotes extensively from Luther.

3. Michael Eaton, *Ecclesiastes*, Tyndale Old Testament Commentaries (Leicester: Inter-Varsity, 1983), pp. 79-80.

4. Herbert C. Leupold, *Exposition of Ecclesiastes* (Grand Rapids: Baker, 1972 [1952]), p. 85.

5. Hengstenberg, *Ecclesiastes*, pp. 104-5.

6. Augustine, *Confessions*, I.1.

7. Hengstenberg, *Ecclesiastes*, p. 121.

Chapter 4: Empty Lives

1. Charles Bridges, *Ecclesiastes* (Edinburgh: Banner of Truth, 1981 [1860]), p. 79.

2. Christian Solidarity International (CSI) has published a world map with a cross entangled with barbed wire superimposed on each country in which state restriction or proscription of Christian work and witness is known to be operative (Christian Solidarity International, Box 24042, Washington, D.C. 20024).

3. Herbert Schlossberg, *Idols for Destruction* (Nashville: Thomas Nelson, 1983). See pp. 59-74 for a challenging review of current concepts of poverty and its cure.

4. Tony Walter, *All You Love is Need* (London: SPCK, 1985), p. 39.

5. Ibid., p. 125.

6. Bridges, *Ecclesiastes*, p. 87.

7. Derek Kidner, *A Time to Mourn, and a Time to Dance* (Leicester: Inter-Varsity, 1976), p. 46.

8. Ibid., p. 52.

9. Herbert C. Leupold, *Exposition of Ecclesiastes* (Grand Rapids: Baker, 1972 [1952]), p. 115.

10. Kidner, *A Time*, p. 52.

Chapter 5: Hollow Religion

1. James Barke, ed., *Poems and Songs of Robert Burns* (London and Glasgow: Collins, 1969), pp. 105ff. The poem, "The Cottar's Saturday Night," is thought to be an evocation of Burns's childhood. Like so many prodigals before and since, Burns had a genuine love and wistful respect for godly parents.

2. Herbert Schlossberg, *Idols for Destruction*, (Nashville: Thomas Nelson, 1983), pp. 232ff. In a chapter entitled "Idols of Religion," the author traces the relationship of church to society in America, noting its parallels with the kind of apostasy described in the Old Testament, particularly in the prophets such as Isaiah. His focus is on the tendency toward "civil religion" that accommodates the cultural norms of a practically godless society. Qoheleth, as we have noted, focuses on the individual's spiritual experience as he relates personally to God.

3. Herbert C. Leupold, *Exposition of Ecclesiastes* (Grand Rapids: Baker, 1972 [1952]), p. 117.

4. Derek Kidner, *A Time to Mourn, and a Time to Dance* (Leicester: Inter-Varsity, 1976), p. 52.

5. W. H. Gispen, *Exodus*, Bible Student's Commentary (Grand Rapids: Zondervan/Paideia, 1982), p. 52.

6. Michael Eaton, *Ecclesiastes*, Tyndale Old Testament Commentaries (Leicester: Inter-Varsity, 1983), p. 97. H. C. Leupold (*Ecclesiastes*, p. 118) thinks only the temple is in view.

7. Robert Leighton, *Commentary on First Peter* (Grand Rapids: Kregel, 1972), p. 291. Robert Leighton (1611-84) was the Archbishop of Glasgow, Scotland, during the period of the Stuart Restoration. His First Peter commentary is one of the classics of biblical exposition.

8. Reformed Presbyterian Church, *The Constitution of the Reformed Presbyterian Church of North America* (Pittsburgh: 1989), p. G-1.

9. Samuel Nesdoly, *Among the Soviet Evangelicals* (Edinburgh: Banner of Truth, 1986), p. 98.

Chapter 6: The Love of Money

1. W. G. T. Shedd, *Sermons to the Spiritual Man* (London: Banner of Truth, 1972 [1884]), p. 374. Shedd was Professor of Systematic Theology in Union Seminary, New York.

2. In 1801, during the naval battle of Copenhagen, Admiral Horatio Nelson disregarded the signal of his superior Admiral Hyde Parker that he withdraw from the engagement. Nelson put his telescope to his blind eye and told Captain Foley, "I really do not see the signal." He won the battle, but "the Nelson eye" became a byword for breaking the rules and getting away with it!

3. Derek Kidner, *A Time to Mourn, and a Time to Dance* (Leicester: Inter-Varsity, 1976), p. 55.

4. *Time*, November 9, 1987, p. 33.

5. Leaving an inheritance for your children is mandated by Scripture, but God has promised to care for those of his children who have no inheritance from their

parents (Ps. 37:25). Furthermore, the parable of the prodigal son (Luke 15:11-24) offers a healthy caution with respect to inheritances and their use and abuse by children.

6. See Larry Burkett, *Your Finances in Changing Times* (Chicago: Moody, 1982) for a helpful in-depth review of personal finances, including the place of savings.

7. Charles Bridges, *Ecclesiastes* (Edinburgh: Banner of Truth, 1981 [1860]), p. 119.

8. Ibid.

9. Michael Eaton, *Ecclesiastes*, Tyndale Old Testament Commentaries (Leicester: Inter-Varsity, 1983), p. 108.

Chapter 7: Learn From Experience!

1. Michael Eaton, *Ecclesiastes*, Tyndale Old Testament Commentaries (Leicester: Inter-Varsity, 1983), p. 109.

2. Rita Nightingale, *Freed for Life* (London: Marshalls, 1982), p. 139.

3. Ibid., p. 140.

4. James W. Alexander, *Consolation* (New York: Charles Scribner, 1853), p. 323.

5. In the Presbyterian system of church government, the "presbytery" is the regional assembly of congregations within its bounds. Pastors and elders are delegated to this body from their local congregations. Among other things, the presbytery oversees the preparation of men for the pastoral ministry and examines them at regular intervals in their course through seminary.

6. Eaton, *Ecclesiastes*, p. 110.

7. Charles Bridges, *Ecclesiastes* (Edinburgh: Banner of Truth, 1981 [1860]), p. 144.

8. Thomas Boston, *The Crook in the Lot* (Swengel, Pa.: Reiner, 1963), p. 64. Thomas Boston (1676-1732) was a pastor in the (Presbyterian) Church of Scotland and famous for his role in the "Marrow controversy" that rocked and revived the Scottish Church. His works are still in print, and his best-known work, *Human Nature in its Four-Fold State* is one of the truly great books of Christian doctrine and piety.

Chapter 8: Wise Up!

1. Psalm 139:7 refers, of course, to the exact opposite. God has promised to be with his people in all their troubles, wherever they are and for their comfort and preservation.

2. Thomas Manton, *The Complete Works*, vol. 2 (Worthington, Pa: Maranatha, 1975 [1871], p. 102. Manton (1620-77) was a prominent pastor and Bible expositor in England. His works fill twenty-two volumes and comprise a full record of his preaching ministry. J. C. Ryle described these as "literary gold."

3. Zophar the Naamithite asks Job, "Can you fathom [by searching, KJV] the mysteries of God? Can you probe the limits of the Almighty?" (Job 11:7). The answer is obvious. Yet man enthrones himself on no more basis than his own empirical interpretation of the world of his senses.

4. Jesus, after his conversation with the woman at the well, takes up this theme with his disciples with the illustration of fields that are ready for harvest (John 4:35-38). God deals with each generation as the farmer does with his harvest. The harvest must be reaped, or the crops will rot where they stand. This is the challenge to every generation of Christians—to reap God's harvest from their own time and generation.

5. Herbert C. Leupold, *Exposition of Ecclesiastes* (Grand Rapids: Baker, 1972 [1952]), p. 162.

6. Charles Bridges, *Ecclesiastes* (Edinburgh: Banner of Truth, 1981 [1860]), p. 173.

7. F. L. Battles comments, in a footnote, on Calvin's use of the same expression in relation to how we are to think of the biblical teaching on predestination. See John Calvin, *Institutes of the Christian Religion*, F. L. Battles, ed. (Philadelphia: Westminster Press, 1960), III.XXI.2.

8. Bridges, *Ecclesiastes*, p. 175.

Chapter 9: Respect Authority!

1. Russ Pulliam, "The Basis for Right and Wrong," *Covenanter Witness*, vol. 103, no. 12 (December 1987), p. 3, (reprinted from *The Indianapolis News*).

2. Michael Eaton, *Ecclesiastes*, Tyndale Old Testament Commentaries (Leicester: Inter-Varsity, 1983), p. 120 n. 1.

3. Canute ruled England from 1016 to 1035. He arrived in England as a pagan Viking raider and died (aged forty) as the Christian King of Denmark, Norway, England, and the Hebrides—"in the odour of sanctity," according to the historian G. M. Trevelyan. An eleventh-century song celebrated his popularity among his Christian subjects:

> Merry sungen the monkes in Ely
>> When Cnut King rowed thereby.
> Row, cnichts, near the land
>> And hear we these monkes sing.

4. Ernest W. Hengstenberg, *A Commentary on Ecclesiastes* (Minneapolis: James and Klock, 1977 [1869]), p. 198.

5. Eaton, *Ecclesiastes*, p. 121.

6. Charles Bridges, *Ecclesiastes*, (Edinburgh: Banner of Truth, 1981 [1860]), p. 206.

7. Ibid, p. 207.

8. Quoted in ibid., p. 205.

Chapter 10: Live in Hope!

1. Scottish schools are still required by law to hold daily worship services and provide religious instruction classes, part of the quid pro quo for the hand-over of the hundreds of church schools to the state in 1872.

2. Michael Eaton, *Ecclesiastes*, Tyndale Old Testament Commentaries (Leicester: Inter-Varsity, 1983), p. 125.

3. In Romans 5:12-21 Paul develops the two themes of sin-condemnation-death (in Adam) and righteousness-justification-life (in Christ) to bring out the meaning of the gospel way of salvation for lost sinners in a fallen world. The juxtaposition between these two themes provides a theological perspective on the conflict of light and darkness for both the individual lives of men and women and the destiny of human history as a whole. Cf. John Murray, *The Epistle to the Romans* (Grand Rapids: Eerdmans, 1968), pp. 78-80.

4. Charles Bridges, *Ecclesiastes* (Edinburgh: Banner of Truth, 1981 [1860]), pp. 215-16.

5. Robert Leighton, *Commentary on First Peter* (Grand Rapids: Kregel, 1972), p. 31.

6. Bridges, *Ecclesiastes*, p. 219. "A sinner has no right," says Bridges, and "a Christian—supported by Divine strength, favour, and consolation, has no reason—to complain. His treasure includes the promise of all that he wants, in a deep sense of his own unworthiness, and of his Father's undeserved love."

7. Eaton, *Ecclesiastes*, p. 127, notes that "this almost Pauline touch [in 9:7] is the nearest the Preacher came to a doctrine of justification by faith."

8. Ernest W. Hengstenberg, *A Commentary on Ecclesiastes* (Minneapolis: James and Klock, 1977 [1869]), p. 215.

9. Eaton, *Ecclesiastes*, pp. 89, 128.

10. John Owen, *The Grace and Duty of Being Spiritually Minded*, vol. 7 in *The Works of John Owen*, W. H. Goold, ed. (London: Banner of Truth, 1965), p. 321.

Chapter 11: Remember You Are Human!

1. M. Wilcocks (*I Saw Heaven Opened—The Message of Revelation* [Leicester: Inter-Varsity, 1975], pp. 100-102) discusses the significance of God's thunders and trumpets in terms of the limits of his patience with a wicked world.

2. Ernest W. Hengstenberg, *A Commentary on Ecclesiastes* (Minneapolis: James and Klock, 1977 [1869]), p. 221.

3. A. J. P. Taylor, *The First World War* (New York: Penguin, 1965), p. 142.

4. Charles Bridges, *Ecclesiastes* (Edinburgh: Banner of Truth, 1981 [1860]), p. 237.

5. Quoted by ibid., p. 239. George Herbert (1593-1633) is one of England's chief poets. His major work, *The Temple*, is an evocation of Christian spirituality through a poetic description of the church building.

6. Derek Kidner, *A Time to Mourn, and a Time to Dance* (Leicester: Inter-Varsity, 1976), p. 92.

7. Michael Eaton, *Ecclesiastes*, Tyndale Old Testament Commentaries (Leicester: Inter-Varsity, 1983), p. 136.

8. Ibid.

9. George Grant, *The Dispossessed: Homelessness in America* (Fort Worth: Dominion Press, 1986), p. 34. This masterly and moving account of modern homelessness argues that this problem is the great unrecognized challenge, in the sphere of practical mercy ministry, facing the church today.

Chapter 12: Invest in Life!

1. The Hebrew *lechem* (bread) is used in Isa. 28:29 for the grain from which the bread is made. See J. A. Alexander, *The Prophecy of Isaiah* (Grand Rapids: Zondervan, 1974 [1875]), p. 459.

2. Charles Bridges, *Ecclesiastes*, (Edinburgh: Banner of Truth, 1981 [1860]), p. 263.

3. F. N. Lee, *The Covenantal Sabbath* (London: LDOS, 1972), pp. 13, 75.

4. Michael Eaton, *Ecclesiastes*, Tyndale Old Testament Commentaries (Leicester: Inter-Varsity, 1983), p. 143.

5. John Flavel, *The Mystery of Providence* (Edinburgh: Banner of Truth, 1976 [1678]), pp. 210-11.

6. John W. Keddie, *Scottish Athletics* (Glasgow: SAAA, 1982), p. 54. In her biography of Liddell, Sally Magnusson records how it was the Christian witness of Eric Liddell that deeply influenced the Christian faith of track historian John Keddie (this writer's brother, now a pastor in Scotland). She relates how this led to

his involvement in the script-writing for the Liddell character in the movie *Chariots of Fire*. See Sally Magnusson, *The Flying Scotsman* (London: Quartet, 1981), pp. 184-85.

7. Ernest W. Hengstenberg, *A Commentary on Ecclesiastes* (Minneapolis: James and Klock, 1977 [1869]), p. 239.

8. Eaton, *Ecclesiastes*, p. 145.

9. Hengstenberg, *Ecclesiastes*, p. 242.

10. Eaton, *Ecclesiastes*, p. 145.

11. Derek Kidner, *A Time to Mourn, and a Time to Dance* (Leicester: Inter-Varsity, 1976), p. 100.

Chapter 13: Remember Your Creator!

1. J. I. Packer, *Knowing God* (Downer's Grove, Ill.: Inter-Varsity, 1973), p. 94.

2. Ibid., p. 92.

3. Ibid., p. 94.

4. Ibid., pp. 96-97.

5. Michael Eaton, *Ecclesiastes*, Tyndale Old Testament Commentaries (Leicester: Inter-Varsity, 1983), pp. 147-48.

6. Charles Bridges, *Ecclesiastes* (Edinburgh: Banner of Truth, 1981 [1860]), p. 286.

7. Ibid.

8. Cornelis Gilhuis, *Conversations on Growing Older* (Grand Rapids: Eerdmans, 1977), pp. 18-19. This wonderful book ought to be read by every young person.

9. F. Kermode and J. Hollander, *The Oxford Anthology of English Literature* (London: Oxford University Press, 1973), 2:2035.

10. The NASB follows the unaccountable rendering of the Septuagint (the Greek Old Testament) to offer "the caperberry is ineffectual." The caperberry was, it seems, a stimulant in some use at that time.

11. "Cryonics" is the process that will allegedly, sometime in the future, revive frozen bodies and give them new lives.

12. Herbert C. Leupold, *Exposition of Ecclesiastes* (Grand Rapids: Baker, 1972 [1952]), p. 282.